As I See It

V.S. RAVI

MANOHAR
2003

First published 2003

ISBN 81-7304-491-0

Published by
Ajay Kumar Jain for
Manohar Publishers & Distributors
4753/23 Ansari Road, Daryaganj
New Delhi 110002

Typeset by
FineCurve Computers,
Meerut City 250002

Printed at
Lordson Publishers Pvt. Ltd.
Delhi 110007

AS I SEE IT

For eighteen years Mr. Ravi, a police officer by profession, has been writing articles on 'science subjects' and has also published four books on science. In this manumental ground-breaking work *As I See It* containing seventy-two thought-provoking delightful essays which have been embellished with quotations from Shakespeare to Stoppard, and Arnold to Attenborough, the author has once again revealed not only his enormous mastery over all branches of modern science, for which he is well known, but also his stupendous knowledge of Shakespeare's plays, his incisive insight into serious issues like the human condition, in the context of man's scientific achievements and moral values, controversial topics like the style of life of Indians settled in America, sensitive questions like 'national integration' and 'terrorism and even general matters of interest to one and all, like movies and sports.

In writing these brilliant articles in his own inimitable, racy and lyrical style, he has generously drawn facts from his own vast store-house of information acquired by him, as a brilliant scholar, a distinguished civil servant and a widely travelled man.

V.S. Ravi, one of the most distinguished police officers in the country, is a scion of the famous Alladi family being the grandson of the Late Sir Alladi Krishnaswamy Iyer, arguably the greatest lawyer of this country has known and regarded as the Chief Architect of India's Constitution. He joined the Indian Police Service in 1963 having graduated in B.Sc. (Hons.) Physics from the Madras Christian College. He has held various important assignments both in Andhra Pradesh and in the Centre. After a brilliant career of 35 years he retired in 1998 as the Principal Secretary to the Government, Home Department, Government of Andhra Pradesh, in the rank of Director General of Police. In recognition of his outstanding performance as Police Officer, he was awarded the prestigious President's Police Medal for Distinguished Service in 1992. (He had earlier been awarded the Indian Police Medal for Meritorious Service in 1985.)

His publications include *Science : The Living Adventure—Astronomy and Space* (1995), *Science : The Living Adventure—Meaning of Science* (1995), and *Science : The Living Adventure—Medicine, Medical Technology and Health* (1999) and *Science : The Living Adventure—Nature and Biology*. This is his fifth book, which in addition to science contains seven scholarly and delightful essays on Shakespeare, which reveal his vast knowledge, of Shakespeare's plays that would stimulate even the layman's interest, in the works of the greatest dramatist of all time, three thought-provoking essays on the human condition, seven incisive articles on life-style of Indians settled in America and some other essays on several general subjects.

To my father
the late V.M. Subramanian of
United Nations whose life and
glorious career have inspired me to
write a book of this nature

What in me is dark illumine
What is low raise and support
That to the height of this great Argument
I may assert eternal providence
And justify the ways of God to men

JOHN MILTON, *Paradise Lost*

Contents

Preface

I am fortunate to have imbibed, retained and fostered from my early childhood the various attributes of science and the enlivening and ennobling influence of art and literature. This has been made possible due to the influence of the scientific attitude and temper, as well as the artistic and aesthetic values displayed by my enlightened grandparents and my parents. My grandfather, the Late Sir Alladi Krishnaswamy Iyer, a legal luminary, an intellectual giant, a renowned jurist, *one of the founding fathers of the Indian Constitution*, and a great connoisseur and patron of art and literature, my revered father the late V.M. Subramanian, an eminent and distinguished engineer, and an international Civil Servant who served the United Nations with distinction for about two and a half decades, and my revered mother Mrs. V.S. Meenakshi, also a great connoisseur of art and literature *have been the source of inspiration for me* to venture into and explore the ever expanding frontier of scientific knowledge and 'the realms of gold' in the words of John Keats.

Recognizing my passion for Shakespeare and my love for English poetry at a very early age my perceptive mother provided me with an opportunity to get the guidance of one of the most knowledgeable professors in the English language in our country, the late Professor N. Balakrishan of Loyal College, Chennai—a teacher, who could recognize in a student genuine love for literature and stimulate his interest further, so as to bring out his full potential. He belongs to a breed that has vanished. Hence, I may be permitted to modestly claim that by the age of fourteen I had been able to acquire a high degree of interest in and association with the plays and poems of Shakespeare and the poetical works of the major English poets.

I also had at an early age the privilege of listening to great scientists like Dirac, Powell, Gamow and Raman and more recently Francis Crick, James Watson, Roald Hoffman and Charles Towns.

My recent forays into the world of scientific journalism are continuing to give opportunity to meet great scientists. I see in every such interaction yet another golden opportunity for a humble student of science like me to feel the pulse and spirit of the giants of science of our times.

The Indian Police Service which I had served with destination for 35 years had given an insight into various aspects of life, society and the state.

The works of some of the greatest poets and writers of the world have fascinated me. Hence in these articles the reader will occasionally find quotations from famous poets which I hope will serve to embellish the arguments spelt out in the essays.

I must confess that the unique contributions, views and utterances of various poets and scientists had become deeply ingrained in my subconscious mind. I have of course identified and acknowledged the source wherever possible. However, it is not unlikely that some of their phrases and expressions have rolled down into my articles here and there without my knowledge because of their total assimilation and synthesis in my mental process. Therefore, while gratefully acknowledging the compelling influence on my writings of the wisdom of the 'Mighty Minds' of literature and science, whose works have added lustre to my essays and have conferred on me a sort of moral sanction to draw from such a vast reservoir of knowledge, though not always at the conscious plane, I apologize if I have unintentionally omitted acknowledging the name of any particular author.

As already mentioned I was inspired at a very young age by the poetry and the plays of Shakespeare and most of the great poetry in the English language.

I wish to thank my father V.M. Subramanian for encouraging me in my study of various books throwing light on the whole gamut of human knowledge at a very early age. I wish to express my gratitude to my mother Mrs. V.S. Meenakshi for giving me a sound classical education and inculcating in me a high sense of idealism and respect for moral values. Thus, even while as a student, I experienced the thrill of reading. English poetry on the one hand and the works of great Telugu poets on the other. I am indeed fortunate to have been born to such noble parents.

I wish to thank my charming wife Jayanthi who despite her heavy work schedule in her office and frequent hectic tours willingly sacrificed her holidays giving up sometimes entertainment and social engagements to create a favourable atmosphere at home to enable me to work on my project. If this gives an impression that she was a mere passive spectator it would be highly misleading and erroneous for I must confess that her constant reminders to me to complete the project, her constructive suggestions and innovative ideas have definitely improved the quality of the final product. Apart from this, the sheer emotional strength her presence gave me cannot be quantified.

I would like to express my love affection and gratitude to my two brilliant and adorable sons Suresh and Arjun, and my lovely and talented daughter-in-law Pooja, whose idealism, enthusiasm, moral courage, and achievements in their chosen professions, have given me the necessary impetus and motivation to undertake this ambitious task. I only hope that these essays render me worthy of my noble family.

I wish to thank my publishers Ramesh Jain, P.P. Jain and Ajay Jain, whose enormous patience and encouragement have sustained in me the necessary enthusiasm to continue to be productive. I am particularly indebted to my good friend B.N. Varma and Bansi Ram who have both taken immense pains to go through the proof of this book at several stages and made many constructive suggestions which have distinctly improved the quality of the articles as well as the format. But for the immeasurably great interest shown by these good friends, I doubt if this volume would have ever taken shape. I owe a great debt of gratitude to all five of them. I apologize to all of them, particularly Varma and Bansi Ram who willingly clarified the doubts I raised several times regarding the format of the book, though I must have disturbed their daily schedule of heavy work.

Man has made spectacular achievements in almost all fields—Science, Technology, Communication, Medicine and even entertainment.

I cannot at this juncture resist recalling the brilliant narration of David Attenborough who in his book 'Life on Earth' sums up in one remarkable burst of eloquence, the entire achievements of man on 'this bank and shoal of time' from the first dawn of creation when he looked up at the sky to the present day when astronauts are soaring into the heights of space in fantastic space ships.

In Attenborough's words . . .

> Homo sapiens has suddenly become the most numerous of all large animals. Ten thousand years ago, there were about ten million individuals in the world. Today there are a few billions. These extraordinary creatures have spread to all corners of the earth in an unprecedented way. They live on the ice of the Poles and in the tropical jungles on the equator. They have climbed the highest mountains where oxygen is cripplingly scarce and dived down in special suits to walk on the bed of the sea. Some have even left the planet altogether and visited the moon.

He further goes on to say,

> Man's passion to communicate and to receive communications seems central

to his success. We do not limit ourselves to our own acquaintances or even our own generation. Archaeologists labour to decipher clay tablets rescued with painstaking care from Uruk and other ancient cities in the hope that some citizens long ago may have recorded a message of more significance than a boastful genealogy of a chief or a laundry list.

He adds

And scientist convinced that man's most refined language of all is that of mathematics have selected a universal truth that they believe will be recognized through all eternity—a formula for the wavelength of light—and beamed it towards other galaxies in the Milky Way to proclaim that here on earth, after three thousand million years of evolution, a creature has emerged that has for the first time devised its own way of accumulating and transferring experience across generations.

And further adds,

This last chapter has been devoted to only one species, ourselves. This may have given the impression that somehow man is the ultimate triumph of evolution, that all these millions of years of development have had no purpose other than to put him on earth. There is no scientific evidence whatever to support such a view and no reason to suppose that our stay here will be any more permanent that of the dinosaur. The processes of evolution are still going on among plants and birds, insects and mammals. So it is more than likely that if men were to disappear from the face of the earth, for whatever reason, there is a modest, unobtrusive creature somewhere that would develop into a new form and take our place.

He winds up his eloquent narrative with a note of caution to mankind. But although denying that we have a special position in the natural world might seem becomingly modest in the eve of eternity, it might also be used as an excuse for evading our responsibilities. The fact is that no species has ever had such wholesale control over everything on earth, living or dead as we now have. That lays upon us, whether we like it or not, an awesome responsibility. In our hands now lies not only our own future, but that of all other living creatures, with whom we share the earth.

V.S. RAVI

PART I

SCIENCE

1. *A Golden Century for Science: The Romance of Physics*

All science is founded on the assumption that the physical world is ordered. The most powerful expression of this order is found in the laws of physics. Nobody knows where these laws came from, nor why they apparently operate universally and unfailingly.

CAROLYN SERIES

As we approach the next millennium, the question that is foremost on every one's mind is as to what man has been able to accomplish on this planet in the present century in the scientific field. Such an assessment is absolutely necessary because there is no doubt that the future historians would definitely regard our century as the Golden Age of Science. It would be no exaggeration to claim that more discoveries have been made in this century than in previous centuries and even the rate of scientific discovery is getting accelerated at a dizzying pace. The exercise to list out the best achievements of man in science and technology in the twentieth century is almost an impossible task. It is like asking a gardener or a florist to pick and choose two dozen best flowers in a huge garden or a park which has thousands of flowers blushing in all hues. Therefore, while selecting scientific achievements which have enabled man (a) to conquer his environment; (b) unravel the mysteries of the universe; (c) improve the quality of his life; (d) extend lifespan by improving man's ability to fight disease, the person making the choice is necessarily handicapped in his unenviable task. However, even among these spectacular achievements that have given man a unique and advantageous place, a modest effort could be made on the basis of qualitative as well as quantitative changes, any particular achievement has brought about in man's quality of life or unearthing any truth or any secret of nature which had hitherto remained undiscovered. One recalls Pope's flattering reference to Newton in this context:

Nature and Nature's Laws lay hid in night
God said let Newton be and all was light.

Let us therefore assess achievements on the basis of the impact they had on human civilization as well as the extent which they have unravelled nature's secrets.

However, before giving our assessment about the progress made in science and technology in this century, it would be desirable to narrate an apocryphal anecdote about the German physicist Max Planck. Max Planck in the beginning of the century had approached his professor in Munich stating that he wanted to take up a career in physics. Apparently his professor had tried to discourage him with the argument that physics had completely been 'wrapped up' and there was nothing left to be discovered! But, Max Planck stubbornly insisted on becoming a physicist ignoring his professor's advice. The rest is history, for shortly afterwards, the two great discoveries—the Theory of Relativity and Quantum Mechanics—shook physics to its very foundations, changing forever our perception of the universe. Thus, almost in every branch of science a general feeling of complacency that everything had been discovered was shaken by new concepts and ideas like never before in history.

To cite an example, in 1900 no one knew Einstein's Mass Energy equation $E = mc^2$, in which 'E' is energy; 'm' is mass and 'c' is the velocity of light. But, in 1950, the atomic bomb, which was a logical outcome of the equation, flattened two cities in Japan.

As Nobel Laureate Sir Peter Medawar said, probably the two greatest triumphs of Science in the twentieth century are Einstein's Theory of Relativity and the discovery of the 'Double Helix' by Crick and Watson. The field that witnessed the most significant gains in the beginning of the century was physics. Logical conclusions and results flowed from the discovery of the Theory of Relativity, e.g. first, nothing can travel faster than light. More correctly according to Relativity it is not possible to cross the speed-of-light 'barrier'.

This would mean that if a particle is travelling slower than light it would take an infinite amount of energy to accelerate it up to the speed-of-light. If a particle did exist that travelled faster than light, it would always travel faster than light. This means that on the other side of the light barrier it would require infinite energy to slow down the particle to the speed of light ! Relativity permits the possibility of the existence of such particles, christened 'tachyons' (particles travelling slower than light are called 'tardons'). The light barrier is some kind of 'threshold' similar to an infinitely long high ridge. As John Gribbin has graphically described, particles on our side of the ridge roll down the slope to slower speeds, but particles on the other side of the slope roll down to greater speeds, unless they are given a boost of energy. As time runs progressively slower as we move towards the speed of light (climbing the ridge) from our side coming to a halt at light speed, time runs slowly backward on the other side of the barrier and more and more rapidly backwards for tachyons more and more rapidly as they descend the ridge on the other side—as they move further away from light speed. This may account for the recent findings of physicist Paul Davies that light had infinite speed at the point of creation and had gradually slowed down stopping at the barrier of 3,00,00 km/sec (the present velocity). Therefore it would be too premature to make sweeping conclusions regarding the implications of the discovery of Davies which should at this stage be viewed only as a refinement of a certain aspect of Relativity. Second, energy and mass are inter-convertible. Third, the classical notions of absolute position and time lost their meaning yielding to the concept of relative distances and times. Fourth, there was no need for physicists to introduce the existence of a luminiferous ether that would imply determination of absolute speeds and distances. Fifth, man lives in a four-dimensional world in which the three-dimensional space is conjoined with an extra dimension of time.

Towards the end of the nineteenth century there was still a lot of confusion about the nature of heat. The entire approach to radiation centred on the question of why the quality of radiation emitted by a hot object changes in a characteristic way as the temperature increases. Though, by the end of nineteenth century, it became clear that all objects emit radiation that spans a spectrum of frequencies that increase as the temperature increases, it was not clear how the intensity of radiation in such a spectrum varied with the frequency. The question was finally answered by Max Planck who postulated that radiation of a particular frequency exists only as 'quanta'. The greater the frequency, the greater the energy of the quanta. Thus, Planck showed that even energy consists of atoms, a fact indirectly proved by Einstein also later by explaining that a minimum frequency (and thus energy) is required to release electrons from metals to produce current.

In 1910, Rutherford discovered that all atoms were constructed from a number of negatively charged electrons and a nucleus carrying a positive electrical charge embodying most of the mass of the atom. Typically, the dimensions of the nucleus are one ten thousandth of those of the atom. The next development occurred in 1913 when the renowned Danish physicist, Niels Bohr, reconciled the properties of the simplest atom, that of hydrogen, with Planck's discovery that energy is transferred between atoms only in quanta. Bohr was able to establish that in the hydrogen atom, electrons travel around the nucleus like planets revolving about a sun, except that only a restricted set of orbits is allowed each with a well-defined energy. Bohr had understood the conditions in which an electron in a tiny hydrogen atom can remain indefinitely in orbit without losing energy. However, at that stage, the behaviour of atoms other than that of hydrogen remained unexplained. While all these developments were taking place, the fundamental question as to how to reconcile that radiation was a wave like phenomenon as had been suggested by Huygens, and the concept that radiation consisted of indivisible quanta was indirectly solved by Einstein himself in 1913, who explained photo-electric effect by using the corpuscular (photons) theory.

At this stage, two famous scientists, Werner Heisenberg and Ervin Schrödinger introduced the radically new concepts of matrix mechanics and wave mechanics respectively to explain many of the phenomena which constitute what is now described as quantum mechanics. While Heisenberg came out with his 'uncertainty principle' (it is not possible to measure the position and speed of a particle at the same time), Schrodinger described mathematically, the properties of quantum systems. Then, Paul Adrain Mauice Dirac, showed that the developments were equivalent to each other. His equations gave fresh mathematical sanctity to quantum mechanics which has since proved to be one of the most remarkable intellectual achievements in the entire history of science, a tool for calculating systems on an atomic scale.

Though some of its implications bordered on the philosophic and mystic, with all its seemingly internal paradoxes, quantum mechanics led to many major discoveries and made possible directly or indirectly most of the fruits of modern technology, including the transistor, the television, etc. Thus, the beginning of the twentieth century for physics was a great period of fundamental discoveries. It is true that technically some of the discoveries were actually made a few years before the new century was ushered in—such as (a) Röntgen's discovery of X-rays in 1895; (b) Becquerel's discovery of radio activity in 1896, which in a sense was a reverse phenomenon of Röntgen's discovery; (c) Plutonium and Radium in 1898 by Mary Curie and (d) Electron by J.J. Thomson in 1897.

The contribution of J.J. Thomson is unmatched in scientific history in the sense that seven of his students including his son went on to become Nobel Prize winners in addition to his own phenomenal contributions to physics. It was left to Rutherford, a student of J.J. Thomson, to describe the structure of the atom on the basis of his various experiments including the one on alpha particle scattering.

2. *A Golden Century for Science: The Revolution in Medicine*

Is it not evident in the last hundred years . . . that almost a new Nature has been revealed to us ? . . . more noble secrets in optics, medicine, anatomy discovered, than in all those credulous and doting ages from Aristotle to us.

JOHN DRYDEN

This observation is relevant to the twentieth century also.

While Physics continued its triumphant march, scientists working on the life sciences were also making a modest beginning. In 1900, the Austrian Scientist, Landsteiner first divided human blood into groups. Adrenaline, a substance secreted by the adrenal gland located near the kidneys was discovered by Jokichi Takamine of Japan in 1901, who also succeeded in synthesizing it. By 1920, work done by two British scientists, Bayliss and Starling prepared the ground for establishing that diabetes was caused by the malfunctioning of the pancreas, a large soft digestive gland resulting in shortage of a hormone called 'insulin'. They discovered the first hormone secretin produced by the pancreas and the perislatic wave of the intentines.

In a major breakthrough, three Canadian scientists, Banting, Macleod and Best, discovered a method to manufacture insulin thus providing a cure for people suffering from that disease. Just before the turn of the century, the importance of anti-toxins and vaccines were realized for checking diseases like, Tuberculosis, Diphtheria and Tetanus.

The stage was then set for stepping up man's fight against bacterial infections. Domagk succeeded in controlling streptococcus with the drug prontosil (sulphanilamide) and other related compounds known as sulpha drugs that proved effective against many types of bacterial infections.

Then occurred probably the greatest development in the history of man's fight against the infectious diseases. A certain substance isolated from a fungus mould by a tenacious and observant British scientist, Alexander Fleming became the first of several generations of powerful drugs to be known as 'antibiotics'.

Penicillin proved effective against a whole spectrum of diseases from Pneumonia to Gonorrhoea. Fleming's discovery in turn led to the discovery of many other such antibiotics all over the world. While Fleming, Florey and Chain became household names for curing the sick, the wounded and the infected by administering penicillin, Selman Waksman soon discovered streptomycin a drug to combat Tuberculosis. Because of these great discoveries, mortality due to pneumonia, and various other life-threatening infections came down drastically.

Vaccines to battle yellow fever, dengue fever, typhus and typhoid were produced. The role of vitamins in preventing certain diseases like Pellagra, Beri Beri, Rickets and Scurvy was recognized and scientists built strong edifices on the foundations that had been laid earlier by such pioneers as Pasteur and Jenner. Mendel's work and the laws of heredity were improved upon but the most spectacular discovery in biology since Darwin's evolution was made in April 1953 by Francis Crick, a British scientist, and Jim Watson of America, who with the help of the X-ray photographs provided by Rosalind Franklin and also some vital data given by Maurice Wilkins discovered the structure of DNA, the genetic code that spells out the secret of life. Except Rosalind Franklin, whose premature death from cancer probably deprived her of the prize, all the other three members of the team were given the Nobel Prize.

In early 1950s, Miller and Urey boiled in a flask all the substances they thought would have been present in the atmosphere of the newly born earth and subjected them to bombardment by ultraviolet radiation.

They simulated conditions that must have existed when life arose on the early earth. The formation of amino acids at the bottom of the flask, showed that they had been on the right track. The study of viruses added a new chapter to Biology and unearthed evidence that so called 'slow viruses' caused Alzheimer's disease, multiple sclerosis and kuru. The recent work of Pruisner in understanding such phenomena is yet another significant chapter in this story. Though, a complete cure for such diseases is still a long way off, drugs have been discovered that can slow down the aggressive march of these crippling ailments and provide relief from suffering.

A drug was found to halt the progress of leprosy and scientists were hoping to get the armadillo to be a source of a new drug to achieve a major breakthrough. In fact, some success has already been achieved in this field.

Advances in pharmacology enabled man to reduce mortality rate due to several diseases. Management of injuries due to accidents as well as treatment and post-operative care in hospitals received a boost.

While the birth control pill liberated women from unwanted pregnancy, new techniques simplified surgical procedures in gynaecology. New methods were found to detect and control blood pressure and assess damage to the heart due to bad eating habits, faulty life-styles or hereditary factors and drugs and surgical techniques introduced to protect the heart from further damage or repair damaged arteries.

Emphasis was laid on better nutrition and the avoidance of harmful fats on the body and heart in particular. The dangers of smoking and pollution were realized sufficiently to make people take precautions early in life.

Calcium channel antagonists, Beta Blockers and Ace-inhibitors were discovered apart from technological marvels like balloon angioplasty and bypass that have saved millions of lives.

The focus shifted to the human brain and neuroscience began to witness spectacular discoveries for the first time in medical history. Aided by sophisticated tools such Computerized Axial Tomography scans, Positron Emission Tomography, Magnetic Resonance Imaging, etc., doctors were able to detect abnormalities at an early stage with a view to finding a cure.

Roger Sperry did splendid work to understand the physiology of the two hemispheres of the brain and explained the phenomenon of split brains while the findings of Hubel and Wiesel threw light on the functioning of the visual cortex—work for which all three received Nobel Prize.

In Gastroenterology, though many old conventional methods of treating ulcers like antacids are still being used for giving symptomatic relief, new drugs called H-2 antagonists and proton pump inhibitors have brought relief to million of people suffering from various kinds of stomach disorders. An Australian doctor, Marshal not only found evidence to suggest that many stomach ailments were due to a bacillus called Helico bacterpylori, but also was able to find a cure for it.

Notwithstanding all these great successes, cancer still remains unconquered. Most Cancers, despite marginal success if detected very early invariably prove fatal. Strains of Bacteria resistant to antibiotics have evolved making old diseases come back in a more virulent form. Thus, the arrival of new drug-resistant germs is likely to cause epidemics, posing a fresh threat. In addition, AIDS (Acquired Immunodeficiency Syndrome) is now sweeping across the globe. Scientists are carrying out research but are not hopeful of finding even a vaccine to check this disease within to the next 20 years, let alone a drug to cure it.

3. *A Golden Century for Science: The Dizzy Heights of Astronomy*

Astronomy is one of the sublimest fields of human investigation. The mind that grasps its facts and principles receives something of the enlargement and grandeur belonging to the science itself.

H. MANN

No one can contemplate the great facts of astronomy without feeling his own littleness and the wonderful sweep of the power and providence of God.

TRYON EDWARDS

One of the fields that benefited from these great advances in physics was astronomy. People, like Walter Sydney Adams, Eddington and Indian astro-physicist Chandrasekhar studied various Stellar phenomena. The so called 'red shift', confirmed Einstein's theories. In 1929 Hubble who was studying galaxies established that the speed of which a galaxy recedes from us is directly proportional to its distance—a finding that enabled him to determine the radius of the known universe (observable at that state) as thirteen billion light years. Chandrasekhar found the limit of the mass of a star above which it cannot become a white dwarf—extraordinary work for which he was awarded the Nobel Prize after about five decades.

At about the same time, Niels Bohr succeeded in drawing up the model of the Hydrogen atom continuing Rutherford's work while Pauli, the Austrian physicist, postulated the 'exclusion principle' which stipulated that once an electron is an orbit, it automatically prevents any other electron from occupying the same orbit. Several major discoveries like theory of the dual nature of light postulated by De Broglie followed. Dirac theoretically predicted the existence of antimatter a fact, experimentally proved by Anderson by isolating the positron. Heisenberg, Schröedinger, Dirac, Pauli Rutherford, De Broglie and Anderson became Nobel Laureates, though ironically Rutherford, one of the greatest physicists of all time was awarded the prize for Chemistry, a fact he did not very much appreciate!

The Second World War necessitated the invention of a new kind of weapon with enormous destructive capabilities. This was made possible by the implications of Einstein's mass energy equation. Scientists were able to split the atom and release enormous energy that could devastate cities. A galaxy of scientists including Otto Hahn, Enrico Fermi, Oppenheimer, James Chadwick, Hans Bethe, all responded to the call of the US Government to design and build a bomb, which finally put an end to the Second World War. However, at least some scientists like Enrico Fermi realized the potential power of the atom in releasing energy for useful purposes also.

Even as Edison the pioneer of about 1300 inventions had used vacuum tubes in 1880 as electronic devices to control the flow of electrons, three American scientists, William Shockley, John Bardeen and Walter Brattan found in 1948 that they could use certain crystals to work in the same way. In this manner, solid state semi-conductor electronics was discovered. This led to a spate of inventions and other discoveries. Every aspect of life—communications, automobiles, aircraft, household appliances—was radically affected. Vacuum tube computers yielded place to the modern computer, which became progressively smaller and powerful. Entertainment has come a long way from the invention of cinematography by Edison. Motion pictures were perfected for clarity of image, sound and depth and the video revolution has brought James Bond to every household!

Creation of Universe

Astronomy has continued to be an exotic subject since the time of Galileo and Copernicus. The behaviour of planets and stars have been studied in greater details and various theories have been put forth to explain the creation of Universe and origin of life. The background hiss of the first explosion that created the universe was picked up by Penzias and Wilson, who both received the Nobel Prize. The 'Big Bang' theory of creation, put forth by Lemaître, Gamow, Bethe and others gained credibility pushing the steady state theory postulated by Hoyle to the background.

Several astro-physicists attempted to explain the creation and existence of universe including Guth, who suggested what is known as the Theory of Inflation.

In the field of particle physics, Carlo Rubia and Simon Van Dermeer used the modern accelerator at the Cern Laboratory in Geneva and discovered the 'W-particle' predicted by the electroweak theory of Steven Weinberg, Sheldon Glashow and Abdus Salam. These scientists as well as Murray Gell-mann who came out with his theory of quarks won Noble Prize for their discoveries.

Black holes are being studied in great detail by England's Stephen Hawking, the greatest living astro-physicist, who is now occupying the world's most prestigious scientific post—the Lucasian Chair in Cambridge, England once occupied by Newton and Dirac. 'A Black Hole is a region of space where the density of matter was once so great that it collapsed under its own weight creating around itself a region from which even radiation cannot escape.' Along with Roger Penrose, Rouse Ball, Professor of Mathematics in Oxford University, England, Hawking is probing deeper into the mysteries of space.

Travel in the beginning of the century created a revolution with the invention of aeroplane by Wright brothers. It has undergone enormous modifications and improvements with today's jets being able to carry passengers across continents in a few hours. Human lifespan has been pushed up to 70-90 years, thanks to man's ability to conquer diseases and better nutritional methods. However, it is unlikely to ever cross the limit of 120 years set by the laws of biology. When all is said and done, considering man's small size and short period of stay on earth, his achievements have to be regarded as truly spectacular. However, he remains basically a vulnerable creature whose life can be ended with an injury on the head, or wrong diagnosis of a disease or improper food habits that provide no resistance against many of the diseases. Therefore, while we can with a great degree our satisfaction pat ourselves on our backs for the many triumphs and victories achieved in almost every sphere of human activity, we should enter the next millennium in all humility and full realization that at any time not only unconquered diseases but also wars arising due to faulty political systems can snuff out human life from this planet. Man's future lies in his own ability to find the right solution to emerge victorious by exploiting the advantages gained during the last one hundred years.

4. *A Golden Century for Science: The Lost Glory of Indian Science*

> If I were asked under what sky the human mind has most fully developed some of its choicest gifts, has most deeply pondered on the greatest problems of life, and has found solutions for some of them which well deserve the attention even of those who have studied Plato and Kant—I should point to India.
>
> MAX MUELLER, German Linguist and Historian on India

Today as the world is getting ready to usher in another scientific revolution, motivated propaganda based on distorted historical facts conveniently put forth to buttress their arguments by certain interested parties has made everyone believe that India is a country of grinding poverty and lack of technological development. What is indeed astonishing is that such an erroneous impression has till now remained unchecked.

It is conveniently forgotten by these myopic historians that India was the richest country in the world before the Moghul and British invasions.

It is absolutely necessary to set the record straight and present the true picture if we are to regain our reputation as a great country blazing a trail for the rest of the world to follow.

India never invaded any country in her last 10,000 years of existence, a truly remarkable indication of her desire to live peacefully in harmony with other nations, while wars had been raging around her all the time.

The first university in the world was established in Takshila in 700 BC. It could impart learning in 60 subjects to about 10,500 students from all over the world.

The University of Nalanda established in the fourth century BC was a great centre for education. All European and Indian languages have sprung from Sanskrit whose range in depth and wealth of literature is unrivalled. The metrical structure and grandeur of the verses of the Vedas and the epics have no parallel in any other language. Indeed, many consider that it is the most suitable language for computer software even today!

India was once the centre of the world for astronomy and mathematics. The number system was invented by India. Aryabhatta, mathematician and astronomer, not only invented the concept of zero, but also introduced many other vital concepts such as the alphabetical system of expressing number, rules relating to square root and cube root, construction of trigonometric sine tables and epicentric models of planetary motion.

He wrote about the rotation of the earth and gave the most accurate value of Pi (symbol) as 3.1416, which was also independently calculated by Budhayana (decimal and place system were known to Indians by 100 BC).

The word Navgatih is the mother of world Navigation; so also the word nov from which was derived the word navigation. The first evidence of navigation can be traced to the river Sind 6000 years ago, long before the Titanic went down after striking an iceberg (Budhayan in the sixth century also explained the famous theory for which Pythagoras is credited with the discovery).

Bhasker Acharya, calculated the time taken for the Earth's revolution as 365.2575648 days long before the age of Smart or Copernicus.

Branches of mathematics such as algebra and trigonometry came from ancient India. Sridharacharya discovered quadratic equations in the eleventh century AD. Greeks and Romans could only conceive of 106 as the largest number whereas Hindu mathematics used number as big as 10 to the power of 53 with specific nomenclatures as early as 5,000 BC.

To quote Albert Einstein: 'We owe a lot to the Indians who taught us how to count without which no worthwhile discovery could have been made.'

Up to 1896 India was the only source of diamond in the world. Even today the great Cullinan of South Africa does not have the romantic aura of the Kohinoor.

India's early advances in the field of medicine were truly remarkable. Ayurveda is the earliest system of medicine known to man. Charaka, the father of Ayurveda, consolidated the discipline 2000 years ago. Another great scientist Sushruta pioneered surgery 2600 years ago. There is evidence to show that many complicated procedures in surgery such as cataract, fractures, plastic surgery, brain surgery, artificial limbs, and removal of urinary stones, were well known to Indian surgeons and physicians who also had an insight into digestion, anatomy and physiology. Over 125 pieces of surgical equipment were known to them as well as the healing power of many herbs, including some which could cure insanity, jaundice and various stomach disorders.

For over a century the world has been worshipping Marconi as the inventor of wireless communication. Now the US-based IEEE (Institute of Electrical and Electronic Engineers) believes on the basis of strong evidence that the true pioneer was Jagdish Chandra Bose and not Marconi.

The first reservoir and dam in the world was constructed in India at Saurashtra. There is evidence to show the earliest man-made lake was also constructed in Chandragupta Maurya's time.

No wonder many western historians and writers are slowly beginning to acknowledge the fact that India is the home of art, culture, literature, and science. Mark Twain regarded India as 'the cradle of the human race, birth place of human speech, mother of history, grandmother of legend and great-grandmother of tradition'.

However, even in the present age though India has received several setbacks due to foreign invasions and a galloping population, we have not lagged too far behind. Our scientists, doctors and engineers are found all over the globe and they are appreciated by all the countries.

India has contributed several great luminaries to the world of science. Mathematical genius Srinivasa Ramanujan, who for sheer mani pulative ability in tangled algebra, does not have a rival except Jacobi and Abel, who belong to another generation. The name Ramanujan in our age and century has become synonymous with mathematics as Einstein is with physics!

Born in a poor family in south India, Ramanujan had to fight adverse circumstances including poverty and lack of opportunity. By sheer luck, he was recognized by England's great mathematician Hardy and invited to Cambridge, where he created mathematical history.

Our greatest contribution to astro-physics is Chandrasekhar. He was the first person to show that when a star has exhausted all its fuel an inward gravitational collapse will begin. This will eventually be halted in most cases by a degenerate gas, i.e. a gas that is completely ionised.

The star will thus shrink into an object composed of material so dense that a match box of it would weigh many tons. He showed that such a star will have the unusual property that the larger its mass the smaller its radius. There will be a point at which the mass of the star will be too great for it to evolve into a white dwarf. He calculated this mass to be 1.4 times the mass of the sun. This is known as the 'Chandrasekhar limit'. It has now been established that all known white dwarfs fall within this limit. Chandrasekhar was belatedly given the Nobel Prize in 1983 along the Willian Alfred Fowler.

Chandrasekhar's illustrious uncle Sir C.V. Raman, discovered Raman Effect for which he was given the Nobel Prize in 1930. He found that when monochromatic light was passed through a transparent substance some of the light is scattered. The spectrum of the scattered light contains weaker lines in addition to the original wavelength. These lines are caused by the loss or gain of energy of photons as a result of this interaction with vibrating molecules of the substance. The Raman Effect is a powerful tool to analyse molecular structure.

Jagdish Chandra Bose was an eminent scientist generally known for his experiments explaining the response of plants to stimuli. What is not widely known is the fact that he is believed to have invented a wireless transmission system before Marconi! He was elected a Fellow of the Royal Society in 1920.

Satyendranath Bose is yet another great scientist. He put forth a theory explaining the behaviour of subatomic particles. His work on quantum statistics applicable to particles with integral spin is also known as Bose-Einstein statistics because of Einstein's association with the same phenomenon.

Meghnad Saha's work on stellar spectra is very useful in determining either the temperature of a star or the relative abundance of the chemical elements being investigated. The Saha equation explains how the various observed spectra of stars are related to their respective temperatures.

Hargobind Khurana was the third Indian to win a Nobel Prize (1968). Following the work of Crick and Watson, molecular biology received a big shot in the arm. The four bases adenine, guanine, thiamine and cytosine present in the DNA chain are read sequentially in groups of three codons—since there are 21 amino and 4 bases, coding was done in the form of triplets.

Khurana succeeded in synthesizing all the 64 codons. His synthesis of the gene is of paramount importance in molecular biology.

Homi J. Bhabha who described the ways of determining the probability of electron-positron scattering in an atom. He is well known for his explanation of the phenomenon of Cascade ray showers in cosmic rays.

Bhabha was a man of vision who supervised India's nuclear energy programme and was the first chairman of India's Atomic Energy Commission.

There are several other bright Indian scientists whose names cannot be ignored such as Vikram Sarabhai, who did useful work on time variation of cosmic rays and set up the space science and technology centre near Thumba. Narlikar proposed the steady state theory of creation of the universe along with Hoyle of English. The theory has been overshadowed by the Big Bang theory of Gamow, Lemaitre and Bethe. George Sudershan's concept of 'Tachyons' particles faster than light has not found favour with the scientific establishment which is not inclined to disbelieve Einstein's view that the fastest speed permissible in the universe is that of light; this aspect has assumed significance in view of the recent findings of Davies discussed in the Romance of Physics.

A new generation of Indian scientists are making their presence felt in the United States and England. The impact of their work has to be watched.

The advent of scientific agriculture has changed the image of India from one of a basket case in relation to agricultural capability into one of a bread basket capable of becoming a major agricultural power in the world.

It was in 1968 that the term 'Green Revolution' came into vogue for referring to the transition to science-based farming techniques, capable of enhancing productivity per unit of land and time. The experience of more than 30 years has shown that given appropriate blends of technologies, input supply services and government policies, our hardworking farmers will help the country to feed itself.

Schools of research that measure up to the demands of the most difficult scientific challenges have sprung up in the country.

Research institutes and universities like Indian Institute of Science or Tata Institute of Fundamental Research, University at Varanasi or Hyderabad, Jawaharlal Nehru Centre for Advanced Scientific Research or Raman Research Institute have churned out very good researchers and their work is published in various international journals.

5. *The Human Condition: The Frontiers of Life*

> Man is an intellectual animal and therefore an everlasting contradiction to himself. His senses centre in himself, his ideas reach to the end of the universe, so that he is torn in pieces between the two without a possibility of its ever being otherwise.
>
> WILLIAM HAZLITT

> One life; a little gleam of time between two eternities; no second chance for us forever more.
>
> CARLYLE

One of the dichotomies that has developed in respect of human achievement is the sharp division between the fruits of man's technological triumphs and his inability to enjoy such benefits because of his own physiological limitations. This does not means physiology has not kept pace with physics and chemistry. While physics and chemistry deal with material objects whose speed or accuracy or capacity of efficiency has been increased enormously, physiology on the other hand has not been successful in pushing up the limit of human lifespan (estimated at 120 years), despite spectacular triumphs in controlling infection and advances in surgery and preventive medicine.

Quality of life has improved and longevity has increased but it is considered not possible to cross the magic figure of 120, which has been achieved only by less than a handful of people on the planet. A few more people may reach the century mark.

The highest average figure even in the most advanced countries is somewhere between 70 and 90.

Anyway, at such an advanced age they cannot enjoy most of the good things of life. No 80-years-old can repeat the feats performed at 25. No Bjorn Borg or Muhammed Ali can recapture the glories of Wimbledon or Madison Square Garden.

Our periodic need for food, water and sleep imposes limits on our activities, notwithstanding advances in travel and communication. Spaceships may go to other planetary systems but barring those which go to the nearest planet or moon, no passenger will live long enough to reach the destination.

If a few couples were to board such a ship only the great grand-children of their great grand-children may be able to reach the destination.

Another aspect is our relative position with respect to animals. Our superior intelligence has enabled us to exploit the environment making us monarchs of this planet. But then our awareness of the inevitability of death casts a pall of gloom over our existence despite our attempts to distract ourselves during the interval between the two bench marks. Animals have no such fear except when the member of a weak species experiences a vague sense of doom before becoming the victim of a predator. Some think we are the only species able to contemplate and plan a sexual experience but that is no compensation for other short-comings. We are the only species with awareness of birth over which we have no choice and death, which we fear constantly.

We inhabit a minor planet revolving round a medium-sized star and an incredible number of improbable events led to the appearance of life. There is no evidence to show we are special. It is just that one faculty called 'intelligence' that has given us an edge over animals. A sudden unprotected exposure to hostile weather conditions or a fluctu-ation in physiological constants or an injury can terminate human life. Under such circumstances we can be sure of only what we experience through our senses, particularly pain and pleasure, which appear so real that we are tempted to banish all philosophical considerations such as the purpose of our existence or how and why the universe was created.

But merely reducing our own pain and that of others and maximiz-ing our own pleasure by exploitation of others is not the right solution. There are positive acts intuitively considered good or kind by all human societies best exemplified by caring for a child in need irrespec-tive of whose it is, yours or your enemy's. The existence of man on this plant, however strange or precarious, finds a rational basis in, and ultimately hinges on, such moral values.

6. *The Best Years of Our Lives: The Human Condition*

Life is made up not of great sacrifices or duties, but of little things in which smiles and kindness and small obligations given habitually are what preserve the heart and secure comfort.

SIR H. DAVY

Better be with the dead
Whom we, to gain our peace, have sent to peace
Than on the torture of our mind to lie
In restless ecstasy. Duncan is in his grave.
After life's fitful fever he sleeps well;
Treason has done his worst: nor steel nor poison
Malice domestic, foreign levy, nothing
Can touch him further.

SHAKESPEARE in *Macbeth*

Macbeth laments that to satisfy his own ambition and attain mental peace he had sent Duncan to the grave where ironically the latter had found tranquillity while he himself was being tormented by nightmares. Macbeth was jealous of the dead Duncan. Macbeth says in another context: 'Life's . . . A poor player that struts and frets upon the stage and then is heard no more: it is a tale told by an idiot full of sound and fury signifying nothing'.

Though Shakespeare makes Hamlet say 'the dread of something after death . . . makes us rather bear those ills we have than fly to others that we know not of' and Claudio says in *Measure for Measure*, 'The weariest and most loathed worldly life that age, ache, penury and imprisonment can lay on nature is a paradise to what we fear of death.'

Some critics consider that the utterances of Macbeth in this context as closest to Shakespeare's own view of existence and human destiny.

The theme of life as a play has fascinated many poets. To me it seems to have only three acts corresponding to the three stages (not seven) of a man's life, the first being the years spent with one's parents, the second when romantic love dominates the scene and the third, the period spent with one's children before the dark curtain descends.

In the title of a movie called 'The best years of our lives', produced several decades ago, each 'word by itself has no profound effect but strung together the phrase creates a stirring image'. However, you cannot define these years as they pass you by silently—the happy days of your childhood, the picnics, journeys, vacations, visits to shops and movies, teenage romances, the period of love and marriage, the first taste of parenthood, the triumphs and defeats of your children in the classroom or on the sports field and the interaction with their friends and teachers.

It is the vividness and reality of this experience that compels us to ask questions regarding the origin, purpose and destiny of man. While referring to science as the most successful and glorious enterprise that human beings have ever engaged in, Nobel Laureate Peter Medawar expresses the fear that science will never be able to answer those questions. He rightly says that to reproach science for its inability to do so is no more sensible than to reproach a locomotive for not performing tasks it was not designed to do. For the very same reason, even though it can soften the blow, science cannot explain the existence of pain, anguish, misery and the humiliation of death, which separates loved ones. Hence it is not to science but to religion and philosophy that we have to turn for solace, if not for answers.

Birth decides the eventuality of death and thus the three act play can only be a tragedy that reduces all the triumphs and achievements of science and technology and the glories of our music, literature and art to nothingness. Under such circumstances, 'the best years of our lives' instead of flooding our hearts with delight, drown them in pathos, making a mockery of nostalgia. For we shall never experience those joys again. Against this sad scenario life is reduced to an insignificant event in the cosmos with its aims and purposes destined to remain a mystery. Then the only justification for our existence is to be found in moral values like kindness and goodness as expressed by Stephen Grellet:

> I expect to pass through life but once. If, therefore, any kindness I can show or any good I can do to any fellow-being let me do it now and not defer or neglect it as I shall not pass this way again.

7. *The Human Condition: A Psalm of Life*

> And fear not lest existence closing your
> Account, and mine shall know the like no more
> The eternal Saki from the bowl has pour'd
> Millions of bubbles like us, and will pour.
>
> OMAR KHAYYAM in the *Rubaiyat*

Till the time of Copernicus it had been believed that the earth was the centre of the solar system. It was Copernicus who first proved that our Earth was a minor satellite going around a medium-sized star called the sun instead of being the centre of the solar system as it was believed to be at the time. Then came Darwin who demolished the primacy of man within his own planet with his theory that man was just the descendant of an anthropoid ape and that only the laws of evolution had given him a pre-eminent place on earth.

Then it was Freud's turn to postulate various theories about our subconsciousness abolishing the primacy of man's brain within himself. All these provided the basis of scientific materialism, which dethroned man from the exalted position in which he had placed himself (of course Freud's theories were, later modified in the light of advances in neuroscience).

Having said that, one of the greatest ironies is that 'upon this bank and shoal of time' life as we know it has not come to our notice elsewhere either in our galaxy or in the cosmos.

This conclusion gains credibility because of the belief that any alien civilization, if it exists, would broadcast its messages on the frequency of hydrogen, the most abundant element in the universe, and if such a communication had been sent it should have reached and been detected by us by now. Since this has not happened it means that life as we know it does not exist at least in the vicinity of our planet Earth.

It seems odd, to say the least, that in the vast immensities of astronomical space in a minor planet, which itself is a mere satellite of a medium-sized star in an insignificant galaxy, a series of extremely improbable events had led to the appearance of a phenomenon called life and it is even more odd that another set of strange biological laws gradually made that primitive life form to evolve into other life forms and finally into a creature that is able to study itself and its environment in enormous detail.

Then the question naturally arises whether there was a purpose in the appearance of this creature and if so what is its destiny in the scheme of things. Why has such an advanced life form, as we flatter ourselves to be, been relegated to a remote corner of an insignificant galaxy in the universe?

There is perhaps no use in patting ourselves on our backs when yet one more law of the universe is discovered or a fine poem is written or excellent musical piece is composed as indications of our purpose or 'supremacy'. No scientific achievement or artistic triumph can compensate for the utter humiliation death inflicts on mortals. One of the many arguments put forth by all great religions as proof of the existence of a benevolent creator is the opportunity to do good and bring joy to others. But then how does this explain the presence of so much sorrow, agony, suffering, pain and evil on earth and the manner in which the cruel hand of death snatches away helpless children or innocent old people.

The stark reality of human experience, particularly pain, makes it extremely difficult to dismiss the whole of creation as a mere illusion, though it is tempting to believe in such an idea. If then religion can only offer some solace and not answers to rationalize human existence, and science cannot provide answers as it is not concerned with such issues the balance of the equation lies in the limited opportunity life, provides on the planet, to do good and contain suffering.

This is exactly where history's handful, who make this task their sole aim in life, provide a meaning to all creation, for no other explanation makes any sense. Only in the actions of a Gandhi or a Mother Teresa, a Florence Nightingale or a Father Damien or a Buddha or Christ does human life rise above the level of a farce and acquire a certain dignity.

> Do all the good you can
> in all the ways you can
> to all the souls you can
> at all the times you can
> as long as you ever can.

J. WESLEY

The best portion of a good man's life is his little nameless unremembered acts of kindness and of love.

WORDSWORTH

8. *The Rise and Fall of Civilizations*

> If the world suffers from mental deterioration or from moral degradation, then something goes wrong at the very root of civilization or culture. Even though that civilization may drag out for a considerable period it grows less and less vital and ultimately tumbles down.
>
> JAWAHARLAL NEHRU

The eminent British Historian Arnold Toynbee had observed that history had a tendency to repeat itself. Events occurring in one part of the world repeat themselves in another region after sometime though there may be variations.

Toynbee's theory had been generally accepted and appreciated by people, including students of history.

There are characteristics, which are universally regarded as essential for a civilization to be described as enlightened. Let us look at some of the great civilizations of the past—Egypt, Babylon, Carthage, Greece and Rome (India and China come under a different category, for reasons to be explained later, and, therefore, not mentioned here).

These qualities are (the placement does not indicate order of importance):

1. A high level of literacy, artistic and scientific achievement.
2. Respect for culture, which in turn creates a favourable climate for literature, art and music to flourish.
3. Attaching importance to education, the acquisition of knowledge and the desire to unravel the secrets of nature.
4. Rejection of commercial hegemony, cyber globalism, McWorld consumerism and taking measures to prevent/cure, television-addiction and Mall-fever.
5. Preservation of spiritual values in the absence of which no enlightenment is possible in the sense that Spengler meant when he spoke about the decline of the West.
6. A democratic economic policy closing the gap between the rich and the poor not in the Marxian sense but in the way wealth, opportunities and other similar entitles are equitably distributed (in other words everybody gets a slice of the pie).

The mere fact that a nation is the most powerful and affluent country in the world at any particular point of time is no indication of its possession of the ingredients mentioned above. An unlimited desire to acquire consumer goods notwithstanding their functional utility becomes an end in itself obliterating the six factors mentioned above. Lack of interest in mathematics and science, indifference to the beauty of poetry and art, ignorance of history combined with easy access to packaged entertainment, which does not teach children anything worthwhile, apart from providing them with thrill and excitement, are the first symptoms that indicate the decline of a civilization, necessitating urgent remedial action.

When Rome had started decaying after having reached a pinnacle of glory, a group of monks rejected what the Romans had loved most (gladiatorial contests, gluttony, and sexual orgies) and decided to preserve only what was good in that civilization such as literary excellence and architectural glories. It is the foresight of these monks in choosing what is referred to as the 'monastic option' by protecting some great virtues that centuries later paved the way for the flowering of European culture and the Renaissance. Other civilizations failed to do this and so withered away. In the case of India and China, this particular problem did not arise, thanks to their uninterrupted tradition of thousands of years of civilization.

Therefore, we should not, as Shakespeare said in *Othello* 'throw the pearl away' (our cultural heritage). Let us preserve our epics, Vedas and scriptures, and the works of our great philosophers and poets and not become slaves of consumerism and infotainment. Let us realize that our gadgets are mere tools to make life easy, but let us be aware of their limitations and the potential harm they can cause to the values perennial in man if they are given the upper hand.

The more rapidly a civilization progresses, the sooner it dies for another to rise in its place.

HAVELOCK ELLIS

The true test of civilization is, not the census, nor the size of the cities, nor the crops, but the kind of man that the country turns out.

EMERSON

9. *The Equality of Man*

> All men are by nature equal, made of the same earth by the same creator, and however we deceive ourselves, as dear to God, is the poor peasant as the mighty prince.
>
> PLATO

People who believe in the relative superiority of one race over another conveniently disregard scientific and historical evidence to propagate their theory. On the other hand they give the following points in support of their contention.

(a) Only the present is relevant. Western dominance in almost every field of human activity clearly establishes the superiority of the Caucasian race.
(b) Wealth, success and power are the only indicator of racial superiority and we all know who possesses them.
(c) A mental test, devised by a man called Binet, which measure what is known as 'Intelligence Quotient' accurately determines the level of intelligence.
(d) Ability to perform certain tasks is a measure of intelligence.

Let us analyse the criteria indicated above.

The first two presumptions are classic examples of sample error. History has shown that though at various period different empires had been considered invincible, not one of them has survived. Egypt, Carthage, Greece and Rome have all had their day—only to disappear into the mists of time. If some historian had focused his attention on the first century AD he would have concluded that the Roman Empire would never decline and fall. Similarly some future historian might find that a nation which is poor and weak today might have once been wealthy and powerful.

In his book *The Mismeasure of Man*, evolutionary biologist Stephen Jay Gould has revealed how in the beginning of the last century a handful of racists deliberately distorted the purpose and results of Binet's IQ tests to keep out of America such as those who in their view were racially inferior. While Binet himself had conceded that the scores do not reflect intelligence but were intended only for identifying the 'learning disabled', an official named Goddard and two others deliberately misinterpreted the scores as a measure of intelligence and were responsible for a colossal misuse of science to restrict immigration into America.

Describing the plight of the prospective immigrants Gould said that their failure to pass a simple 'memory test' was due to lack of knowledge of English, fear, confusion and weakness after a long voyage by ship to a strange land rather than due to stupidity. On the other hand Goddard attributed the failure to low intelligence and he enforced a series of measures that did incalculable harm to millions of people.

(a) Those considered absolutely inferior (mostly from Eastern Europe) were denied entry. God only knows how many Einstein's were sent back. Among those who gained entry, measures like sterilisation were employed to prevent in-breeding of those considered to be morons. Another entity called 'mental age' was introduced on that scale, the average for Whites was 13.08, whereas Poles got 10.74 and the Negro 10.41.

(b) The IQ tests as interpreted by men like Goddard were obviously flawed. How else could one explain Faraday getting 10.5! Probably your neighbourhood electrician would get 150.

The question of superiority in performing tasks as a mark of intelligence is discussed by anthropologist Jared Diamond in his book *Guns, Gems and Steel*. Diamond says: 'New Guineans tend to perform poorly at tasks that we have been trained to perform since childhood and that New Guineans have not. Hence when unschooled New Guineans from village visit towns they look stupid to westerners. Conversely, I am constantly aware of how stupid I look to New Guineans when I am with them in the jungle at simple tasks (such as following a jungle track or erecting a shelter) at which New Guineans have been trained since childhood and I have not.' Earlier he says 'At some tasks that one might reasonably suppose to reflect aspects of brain function, such as the ability to form a mental map of unfamiliar surroundings they appear considerably more adept than Westerners.'

So what lessons do we draw from all that has been said above? It is the message that Lincoln conveyed at Gettysburg in 1863, which unfortunately men like Goddard did not heed. We cannot blame Lincoln for this. Fortunately today's America, the greatest democracy on Earth follows Lincoln's ideals more than any other nation. It is a country where justice and freedom are held sacrosanct and true talent is rewarded, a nation that has no place for prejudice based on race, caste, creed and colour. This is an ideal all countries must strive for while shaping their destinies.

Nations will rise and fall, but equality remains the ideal. The universal aim is to achieve respect for the entire human race, not for the dominant few.

CARLOS P. ROMOLO

10. *The State of Science in India: Bureaucratic Fetters*

> An administrator in a bureaucratic world is a man who can feel big by merging his non-entity with an abstraction. A real person in touch with real things inspires terror in him.
>
> MARSHALL McLUHAN in a letter to EZRA POUND

It is unfortunate that our country which gave birth to great philosophers, mathematicians, scientists, saints, sages and poets is today devoid of scientific achievements and technological triumphs. This state has been mainly brought about due to the short-sightedness of our civil servants who are armed with enormous administrative and financial powers. But instead of creating a healthy climate for science, they have decided to put fetters on scientific research, due to misconceptions. (There is no need to cause unnecessary offence by specifying the particular branch of civil service I am referring to for the members of this service can easily recognize themselves; the shoe belongs where it fits.) Therefore, when the world is poised to usher in the revolution in science in the new millennium, our country is not in a position to take advantage of the situation.

Technological developments in this century have taken a quantum leap. If somebody were to go to sleep in the 1900 and suddenly wake up like Rip Wan Winkle today, he would see developments beyond his wildest fantasies. He would be astonished to see people watching movies on television, talking to each other on telephones, cellular and mobile phones, computers and aeroplanes. He would find himself in an entirely different planet full of technological marvels. Man in this century has revolutionized agriculture, communication, travel, and entertainment and has developed computers that have shrunk the scale of astronomical and geological time. He has been able to conquer all kinds of diseases, perform surgical miracles and rectify congenital defects, which would have been impossible for surgeons of earlier generations.

However, what he would not fail to notice is that while thanks to the developments in communication and travel, though our country, like most other countries is enjoying the fruits of modern science and technology, no major contribution has been made by our scientists to this scientific age barring a few exceptions.

Why is it so? Despite hundreds of educational institutions that have mushroomed all over the country during the last 75 years, not a single great theory or discovery has come out from our laboratories (Raman, Chandrasekhar, Bhabha, Saha, Bose are a few exceptions). Why is it that every year when the names of Nobel Laureates are announced, the list consists almost entirely of Americans who get the lion's share followed closely by England, Germany, France and Switzerland or Austria. In fact, since 1901, America, England and Germany have taken the major share of the Nobel Prizes. But our country can boast of only three Nobel Prize winners in science. Of these three, some people may not regard Chandrasekhar and Khurana as products of our institutions alone as they benefited from association with other academic centres also.

Why are we behind, even though our educational institutions are churning out graduates in the various scientific disciplines every year?

The answer is that there is something basically wrong with our educational system, which does not foster the healthy development of the study of science. The result is, learning is reduced to a routine job and our universities are merely manufacturing graduates like 'silicon chips' to be exported to 'factories abroad, mainly to the United States and other developed countries. On the other hand, some brilliant people are also taking up careers in the civil service and avoiding science mainly because civil service offer more comforts than in professionals Sectors! Thus, while on one hand we are exporting graduates to other countries, on the other we have simultaneously created a nation of 'glorified clerks' who are satisfied with some brilliant performance at college level and later continue to perform routine administrative work throughout their working lives.

There are several other factors also which are responsible for this sorry state of affairs. Firstly, most of our civil servants suffer from what is called the 'one visit syndrome'. A civil servant goes for training or to attend a conference abroad, visits a laboratory or university for a day or two. He comes back feeling that he knows everything about the university and begins to advocate what he thinks is the right method of training young people in universities or how to run a laboratory.

It does not occur to him that a mere day's visit to great institutions like Cambridge, Oxford and Harward will not give a clear idea about the atmosphere of these centres. In those universities, even the old halls, ivy branches and windy corridors breathe the air of science. The very walls still resound to the voices of some of the greatest scientists in history. In the Great Court in Trinity College, Cambridge, England, there is a place where Newton first measured the velocity of sound and nearby in a hall there is a marble statue of Newton. There is a place where Rupert Brooke wrote 'The Old Vicarage of Grantchester' and the bridge where Thomas Hood wrote the 'Bridge of Sighs'. The pulse of such great universities cannot be felt in a day. At least a few months are required to get an insight into the functioning of such universities. This is what is lacking. In Cambridge or Harvard, you may accidentally run into Stephen Hawking or Glashow while joining others in a queue for your cup of tea. They would be just standing behind undergraduate students without drawing undue attention to themselves. No bureaucratic fetters stifle the freedom of these great scientists who in an ideal academic atmosphere pursue research single-mindedly with total concentration devoid of constraints. Nor are scientists interested in cultivating the goodwill of a senior bureaucrat or politician, as in our country.

11. *The State of Science in India: On Bureaucrats Advising Scientists*

There is nothing which cannot be made a mess of again by officials.

KONRAD ADENAUER

A civil servant in country very often stops learning about new ideas and developments in science as well as other fields after coming out of the competitive examinations. His horizon does not extend beyond the year in which he had passed the competitive examination! This kind of myopism is reflected in every sphere. Combined with this is an obstinacy that prevents him from keeping an open mind which is essential when new facts in science are presented. Of course, there are a few knowledgeable civil servants who do keep in touch with modern developments. But this is an exception.

Another feature is the practice of making civil servants heads of educational institutions by virtue of their rank. This puts them in a position to sanction grants or funds for a laboratory or an institution.

Instead of asking scientists for their requirements, these civil servants, who merely have administrative control rather strangely take it upon themselves to give 'advice' to such eminent persons as to how they should go about their work.

Media reports reveal that this is the only country in the world where a civil servant or a politician advises or exhorts scientists to work harder or to perform experiments more accurately. It is absurd on the part of a civil servant or politician to advise talented scientists as he is not competent to do so. No dignitary or civil servant abroad would patronizingly tell a professor in Oxford or Cambridge in England or Harward or Princeton in America to work harder or even set targets for him.

Some of our civil servants very often regard scientists as specialists who know less and less of more and more, leading to a stage when they know nothing about anything. By the same argument a bureaucrat can be viewed as a 'generalist' who knows more and more about less and less and therefore reaches a stage of knowing everything about nothing.

Without engaging in such semantics, I would like to emphasize that a civil servant or a politician has no right to lecture to a scientist.

As a civil servant I have noticed this kind of presumptuous attitude on the part of many of my colleagues for 35 years and my only advice to them is to refrain from 'advising' scientists on what they should do. It is enough if they render some financial or administrative assistance when specifically requested.

Our civil servants suffer from a number of misconceptions since they are not in tune with the latest scientific developments. One of my senior colleagues was of the view that jaundice can be cured by making a patient lie down on a white sheet made wet by a donkey's urine! It was his opinion that the bile would descend from the patient's body into the bed sheet making him free of jaundice; another colleague once told a young student that the eyes of a dog glow in the dark because of the presence of phosphorus in the eye-balls. Had he consulted a doctor or a zoologist, he would have been corrected. I wish to cite two more instances which would illustrate what I have been stating. A few years ago, I was listening to a lecture on pulsars by the Nobel Laureate Anthony Hewish. Pulsars are among the farthest objects in the universe used for extremely accurate measurement of time. Anthony Hewish had before him, a slide projector provided by the institution where he was giving the lecture. To enable the audience to see the slide he had to look for a dot on the top of the slide. Unfortunately, this proved a nerve-racking exercise for the technician concerned who desperately struggled for almost half an hour in vain to locate the dot. So there, in front of a defective projector, looking helplessly stood, one of the greatest cosmologists of the century who had successfully located the farthest objects in the universe!

Yet another illustration is the manner in which a very famous dignitary who came to inaugurate a conference of scientists suddenly branched off from the main theme to observe that there are 'many things which mathematics or science could not explain'. First of all it was not clear why he had descended into this ridiculous line of thought. Secondly he started working out on the black board 1 + 2 + 5 = 8, 2 + 2 + 2 + 2 = 8, 3 + 3 + 2 = 8, 2 + 1 + 2 + 3 = 8. According to him it was a puzzle as to how all the four series could add up to 8 and he wanted to know whether mathematics or science could explain such a phenomenon! It was a question which was not only meaningless but totally absurd and beyond the comprehension of any prudent intelligent man. With great difficulty and restraint a few members in the audience as well as scientists attending the function could refrain from bursting into laughter.

Some of our so-called dignitaries do not exactly enhance their own image in the eyes of distinguished men of science from foreign countries who visit our country. Fortunately, they still have respect for our country because of its ancient tradition, history, culture and art. It is rather ironical that this land of Valmiki and Vyasa, Aryabhatta and Charaka should have now descended so low that it has not produced a single great star in the scientific firmament, and on the other hand now produces mediocre men who confuse pseudoscience and superstition with real science. Again I am not referring to a few extraordinary people who have contributed greatly to science and technology. They are exceptions and have already left our country creating a vacuum.

Therefore, our civil servants should refrain from advising scientists, doctors and engineers in respect to their work. It is rather unfortunate that in our country, while on one hand we have a large number of civil servants who think it fit to advise scientists merely because of some rudimentary association they may have had with a particular subject, on the other hand there is also another anomalous situation of a scientist being put in charge of the administration of an educational institution or a hospital, with the result, he stops being a scientist and tries to behave like a civil servant. It is pathetic to see a scientist who had acquired fame for some good quality work done in the past being made to head a laboratory to do routine administrative work.

12. *The State of Science in India: Bureaucracy in India*

A difficulty for every solution.

LORD SAMUEL

When scientists put forth great ideas, people rooted in superstition and convention generally show resistance to such ideas. While good traditions are desirable, ignorance and superstition need to be shunned. History is replete with example of great scientists who have had to get out of the beaten track to voyage through strange seas of thought alone and come out with fantastic ideas or hypotheses which were condemned by conservative people.

When the great physicist Galileo said that the earth moved round the sun, many did not believe him and he was tried before the inquisition and made to confess his guilt and mistake. After he was acquitted, Galileo muttered to himself 'but the earth does move'. There is something that touches the helm of divinity in the utterance of an old Galileo who does not hesitate to speak the truth even in the face of torture and adversity. Such is the stuff of which great scientists are made.

We too had in the past such people but now people of such calibre are rare, thanks to our educational systems which are merely geared to produce hundreds of civil servants.

The competitive examinations merely succeed in creating a group of people who are educated far beyond their capacity for analytical thought and original ideas. This has resulted in all kinds of aberrations; like the ability to use computers is taken by them to be a sign of intellectual manhood (to use Nobel Laureate Medawar's phrase), and their association with politicians lulls them into a false sense of omnipotence. At parties and social gatherings, they like to indulge in an exercise of name-dropping intended to create an awe-inspiring impression of their supposed proximity to seats of power, not to mention their liberal use of modern business management terms and computer jargon carefully calculated to create a good impression of their educational level.

When Charles Darwin propounded the theory of Evolution and the survival of the fittest, he got into a close conflict with the views of the Church. In one of the most famous debates in scientific history, Bishop Wilberforce asked Darwin's friend Huxley if he would like to claim descent from an ape on his grandfather's side or his grandmother's side. In what is perhaps the greatest repartees in the history of science, Huxley told Wilberforce in a packed hall that if he were to be asked to choose between the lowly ape of meagre intelligence and stooping gait and a man such as the Lord Bishop who endowed with great intelligence and education would prefer to prostitute these gifts in order to ridicule those who sincerely try to seek out the truth, he would without hesitation choose the ape! It was again Huxley who on hearing that a riding accident had claimed the life of Bishop Wilberforce (his head had hit the ground when he fell down and he died) remarked that the Bishop's head had at last come in touch with reality and as he had expected the 'consequences were fatal'.

We enjoy the fruits of science and technology, but never bother to ask how the technology operates. Bureaucrats travel routinely by aeroplanes but they never give a thought as to how such a heavy mass of metal gets airborne, provide all modern comforts and amenities and crosses the entire globe within a span of 24 hours. A child these days merely switches on the video or television to see a film. The thought as to how a picture appears on the screen would not occur to the child. It is we who have spoilt the curiosity of the child, the eagerness and the intelligence. What modern technology has done is to cloy the hungry edge of scientific curiosity. Why should a child bother to ask/know how a television works if without any effort on its part, the father, a successful civil servant, buys the child a television set at a very young age. One the other hand, one would find it strange to realize that even great scientists do not hesitate to ask simple questions.

The science museum in San Francisco has thousands of exhibits each of which works on a certain scientific or mathematical principle. It has been noticed that among the visitors who come there everyday are a large number of eminent scientists, including Nobel Laureates. A casual visitor would spot a couple of Nobel Laureates explaining a simple scientific phenomenon rather enthusiastically to a young student or visitor.

Civil servants suffer from several misconceptions. The first rising that old scientific theories are always disproved by new theories. Science is very often the refinement of old theories. Isaac Newton thought light was a particle and explained some phenomena based on that assumption. On the other hand, Christiaan Huygens assumed that light behaved like a wave and explained many phenomena like diffraction and interference. Albert Einstein could explain the photo-electric effect only by assuming the particle nature of light. Interestingly, Einstein bagged the Nobel Prize for his explanation of photo-electric effect and not for the General Theory of Relativity which revolutionized physics.

The second misconception is that scientific discovery largely depends on luck. There are scores of examples to disprove this. Alexander Fleming's discovery of Penicillin is believed to have been the offshoot of luck. Fleming had, from the beginning, been looking for an agent that could kill bacteria without harming human tissue. The popular version of his discovery goes as follows: A famous English scientist had accidentally left behind a plate containing fungus mould and on the next day he had discovered that a colony of bacteria adjacent to the plate had been wiped out. He had thus established a definite correlation between the presence of this mould (Penicillin) and the destruction of the bacteria. It is conveniently forgotten by most people that Fleming, in fact, had been feverishly searching for several years for some powerful agent or drug that could destroy bacteria, without harming human tissue.

The fact is that all the essential ingredients necessary for a major breakthrough—an astute and patient investigator, a well-equipped laboratory, an ideal academic atmosphere and the necessary motivation—were all there. However, as rightly observed by Medawar, Penicillin unlike other antibiotics, destroys bacteria by interfering with a process peculiar to bacteria—the synthesis of the structural element of the bacterial cell-wall.

The non-formation of the cell-wall increases the internal pressure to such an extent that the bacterium growing inside bursts like a balloon which cannot expand further. The cells in the human body contain only membranes and not walls; hence they are protected from damage.

Therefore if at all there was an element of luck, if lies in the fact that the antibiotic Fleming discovered had both the qualities he was looking for; other antibiotics as Medawar observes are terribly toxic because they arrest the growth of bacteria by interfering with metabolic processes of a kind bacteria have in common with higher organisms. Penicillin is not so toxic as it interferes with a synthetic process peculiar to bacteria, normally the synthesis of the bacterial cell-wall.

Hence, they would not exactly have, satisfied Fleming's criteria.

13. *The State of Science in India: Straightening Bureaucracy*

> Nothing in all the world is more dangerous than sincere ignorance and conscientious stupidity.
>
> MARTIN LUTHER KING

One good example to disprove the misconception of the Indian bureaucracy that scientific discovery largely depends on luck is the case of Nobel Laureate Paul Dirac, one of the greatest English physicists since Newton. Having been unable to go to Cambridge owing to financial reasons, he had to remain at Bristol to pursue his studies. Luckily a fellowship given in 1923 enabled him to move to Cambridge. Just when he was about to start his study at Cambridge, he had access to a paper containing a new development in Physics, called Quantum Theory, thanks to his teacher Fowler. The rest is history, for Dirac became one of the pioneers in quantum mechanics. One wonders whether a man like Dirac would have had the inclination or even opportunity to tap his own potential for doing research in science, had even one of these factors which had brought him into the main scientific arena, been missing.

Another instance of luck that one can think of is the team work of Crick and Watson in discovering the DNA structure. Both of them were brilliant but while Watson represented the dynamic approach of American scientists, Crick represented the quintessentially conservative approach of the English school. They both happened to be in Cambridge at the same time and they had access to certain X-ray diffraction plates given to them by Rosalind Franklin who unfortunately did not immediately see the implications of the pictures. Luck and genius, which brought these two great men together, led them to the discovery of the double helix.

Another misconception of civil servants is the belief that science appeals only to reason unlike poetry, music and art which according to them appeal to our aesthetic values. This is erroneous. Like all great disciplines, science also dwells on beauty as well as on reasoning. The great Dirac once said that it is important to have beauty in an equation rather than mathematical correctness. He was able to see beauty in the way particles behaved and the way the mathematical figures adjusted themselves in an equation. Just as Keats found that truth and beauty are one and the same, scientists depend on their rational faculties as well as their aesthetic sense for their equations and experiments. By the same token here is no justification on the part of some bureaucrats entertaining fears about scientific research going haywire and out of control if limitations are not imposed. They rather illogically argue that if biologist are given too much freedom they may end up producing undesirable creatures and monsters.

This argument is not only erroneous but also misleading as there is no case for stifling freedom of scientific research in a democratic society. Scientists are only interested in knowing the truth. They are not interested in the 'how' of things. After their discoveries, some people may manufacture undesirable products based on these discoveries in addition to manufacturing hundreds of useful things. If bureaucrats want to discourage the manufacture of a certain product, they can always do so but society cannot take upon itself the task of putting permanent fetters on scientific research. If scientific research had been fettered the world would have had no Archimedes, or Copernicus, no Galileo, Newton, or Einstein. Fears entertained by bureaucrats and politicians that the next generations will breed dangerous monsters are also similarly unfounded.

Yet another absurd misconception that science and technology are synonymous. These two are as different as Newton and Eastman Kodak, Babbage and Bill Gates, Pasteur and Glaxo Laboratories. Without belittling the impact of technology in society or their importance, one has to differentiate between someone who does basic research in fundamental science and another who merely engages in its mercenary exploitation. It has never ceased to amaze me as to why civil servants, who are supposed to be intelligent people, cannot see this basic distinction and confuse one with the other.

Civil servants especially must realize that it is our knowledge of mathematics, physics, engineering and space travel, medical science and chemistry, and more than anything else our passion to communicate and receive communications, that have given as a pre-eminent place in the scheme of things. Let us not allow bureaucratic short-sightedness, ignorance and obstinacy make us fritter away the evolutionary advantage gained by several thousands of years of development.

That automatically lays upon all the civil servants in our country whether they like it or not the awesome responsibility of not only having to escape the dictates of their narrow vision and misconceptions but also to create a favourable environment for the benefit of our scientists and thus help the country.

14. *Whither Science?*

> What are the sciences but maps of universal laws; and universal laws but the channels of universal power; and universal power but the outgoings of a supreme universal mind!
>
> E. THOMSON

Over the past few years there has been a gradual erosion of interest among students in great works of literature partly due to the influence of television, video and the cinema, lack of enlightened teachers in our educational system and also a misplaced emphasis on examination results which do not give a student the opportunity to experience the thrill of great poetry or prose.

It is seen that the same situation prevails in respect of science also. Let us first define science, its purpose and limitations. Science represents the best mental discipline that man has at his command to understand the laws of the physical universe. It is all about questions and answers, putting questions to understand a partial phenomenon, it comes out with the best possible answer based on logic and experimental observation. And these answers remain the same whatever the frame of reference, wherever the experiment is performed and irrespective of the person carrying out the experiment. But the entire process starts with a question arising basically out of curiosity, e.g. why does an apple fall to the ground or why is the sky is blue? It is this curiosity which drives the scientist to search for a plausible explanation.

It may be mentioned that children also have the same curiosity when they begin their journey of life; they are full of curiosity and keep asking questions, some of which even adults cannot answer. Instead of trying to find answers for such questions adults snub such children. In fact, what distinguishes the curiosity of the scientist from that of the child is that the former's questions are more structured and organized. Nor is the scientist put off by failure. What characterizes his method is a certain persistence that does not allow him to forget the question till he has found an answer.

But as far as children of today are concerned it is we adults who are to be blamed. If the child can, by operating a small 'remote control' switch, see hundred channels in a TV in one minute how will he have any interest in finding out how a television or video works. No adult has the patience or knowledge to explain how an aeroplane takes off or lands. Too much of excitement (in particular, entertainment) robs the child of all curiosity and incentive to learn.

Here again, as in great works of literature, we need an environment in which the healthy curiosity of a child is encouraged and not killed. What we need is educational science films, not just cartoons of Popeye or Donald Duck; toys based on scientific principles and films and books that outline the stories of some of the greatest discoveries and inventions of our age.

This brings me to my next point. What has happened to all the quiz programmes we used to have in our school days? Being part of your college team, which won a small trophy, was a great source of pride. We still have quiz programmes but of the 'wrong kind' in which the reward for winning is a crore of rupees preventing and defeating the whole purpose.

Discussions in parties dwell on the political situation in the country or the latest movies released. What has happened to all those friendly, scientific riddles for which everyone used to try to find solutions?

Fortunately, some pockets of such interests do exist here and there. I was myself present at a party recently where all took part enthusiastically in finding answers to two such riddles. The first one was as to how one's image gets 'inverted' in a mirror whereas top and bottom, i.e. head and legs, don't get 'reversed'. This occurs because the mirror takes in incoming light and shoots it back at you, thus reversing the direction of the light! You and your image are looking in opposite directions. The question of left or right or up and down does not occur. For the latter to occur you have to place the mirror over the head or stand near it on the floor! The second riddle was more interesting. How is it that we humans have to brush our teeth constantly irrespective of what we eat to maintain oral hygiene whereas lions and tigers do not have to do so—they do not even wash their bloodstained teeth. I have yet to come across a dentist who can answer this question, but the answers to such question represent the very stuff of science.

15. *Science and Belief*

> Science corrects the old creeds, sweeps with every new perception our infantile catechisms and necessitates a faith commensurate with the grander orbits and universal laws which it discloses.
>
> EMERSON

There is an anecdote concerning Paul Dirac, the greatest British scientist since Newton, and one of the founding fathers of Quantum Mechanics. The physicist was apparently sitting in his office, when some research students visited him. As Dirac was a man of few words, one of the students attempted to break the ice, by declaring that it was raining outside. Dirac got up from his chair opened the window, had a peep outside and softy agreed 'Yes, it is'.

What would have appeared as strange behaviour on the part of a great physicist actually represents the quintessential aspect of science—the principle, 'Don't take anybody's word for it', which incidentally also is the motto of the oldest and most famous scientific society, in the world, the Royal Society of London.

Nobel Laureate Sir Peter Medawar, one of the greatest physiologists of the previous century, had said that in fulfilling its declared intentions science is incomparably the most glorious enterprise human beings ever engaged upon. The hallmarks of this mental discipline are: (a) Precise measurement and accurate observation of nature's phenomena; (b) An unbiased attitude of the observer who does not allow subjective views to distort or misinterpret results; (c) The sanctity attached to controlled study that automatically involves the inclusion of 'placebo' in as far as experiments in Pharmacopoeia is concerned; (d) The 'consistency' of results irrespective of the observer and that too in 'independent frames' of reference. A medical system say 'X' can be granted the status of a science only if all these four criteria are present. Otherwise, it has to be considered as mere 'guess work'. It is for these reasons that any medical system which does not meet the four criteria mentioned above cannot be classified as science and has to be rejected. There is no need to specify the systems of medicine. The shoe belongs where it fits. Therefore any medical system which depends on unverifiable claims of having been able to cure some all kinds of diseases in respect of which other systems are said to have failed cannot be categorized as a science. Several medical systems have begun to make fantastic claims of being able to cure all diseases under the sun—from Asthma to Cancer. The crucial point to be remembered is that all these systems have not even a minor insight into human anatomy or physiology but borrow ideas liberally from the only scientific system 'X'. Let us take a practitioner of a system of medicine known as 'Y'. He does not know the difference between the Sigmoid and the Caecum or the ascending colon or the descending colon. Nor is he aware of the various physiological constants or the causes and effects of their fluctuation.

How can he call himself a medical practitioner or worse set up a clinic to cure the sick? Yet he borrows material from textbooks of medical system 'X' which amounts to theft and fraud. Yet another practitioner of a system 'Z' crushes Penicillin and includes it in a 'halwa'-like preparation and passes it off as an ancient cure for a respiratory ailment. The concoction will naturally work but there is no need to explain to the reader why it will be effective. So is the case of Viagra. As unscrupulous pharmaceutical company crushes it and mixes it with the other ingredients of a bogus medicine in capsule form names it 'missile' or 'bullet'. Any effect it has in due to the Viagra—the result capsule outsells Viagra!

Hence, the question of 'believing' in curing or healing, outside the framework of scientific criteria does not arise. This is exactly where many educated persons, including bureaucrats, make a colossal blunder when they declare their belief in some medical system which does not depend on scientific criteria. By the same token they make an even bigger mistake when they reject efficacy the of a science built laboriously over the centuries by studying every human organ in detail analysing diseases and finding cures aided by medical technology and modern pharmacopoeia. No health department of any Government machinery should or can afford to club all these systems and thus cause untold harm to the people.

16. *Science and Technology*

> Any sufficiently advanced technology is indistinguishable from magic.
>
> ARTHER C. CLARKE

Science and Technology are two human enterprises, which though no doubt interrelated, are often confused with each other. The purpose of science is to unravel the mysteries of nature, discover its laws and find out the 'how' of things. It is not concerned with the 'why' of things. It cannot be reproached for its inability to perform a task which it is unsuited to deal with, just as you cannot reproach an automobile for not being able to fly like an aeroplane.

Technology, on the other hand, is the visible end-product you obtain by applying the laws of nature discovered by science, for instance, by constructing an instrument or a machine.

Thus, the laws of physics fall within the purview of science and the application of these laws to launch and regulate satellites would fall within the ambit of technology. Likewise, quantum theory is pure science whose applications led to the invention of various devices like transistors, which would be viewed as technology. Similarly, the elucidation of the structure of the DNA molecule is quintessential science whereas the development of techniques to handle human disorders by manipulation of genes may come under the purview of medical technology.

We cannot deny the achievements of 'technology', an enterprise that has enabled man to derive immense benefits in almost every field of human endeavour. Television that beams programmes round the clock all over the globe, sophisticated medical diagnostic procedures like MRI, CAT scan, etc., are examples of technology that have immensely improved the quality of our lives.

But we must not lose sight of the fact that without the discovery of basic scientific principles, no technological breakthrough could have been made except of course through sheer chance.

Our modern day executives, business magnates and even computer programmers who bandy about jargon like 'user-friendly', 'download', 'password', 'floppy discs' at the drop of a hat would do well to remember that the whole edifice of computer technology would not have come into being but for pioneers of science like Faraday and Maxwell laying the foundations of electromagnetic theory. The average person is so bedazzled by technology, the end-product of science, that he seems totally oblivious of the scientific insights and principles on which it is based.

So entrenched is this attitude, namely, the adulation of technology and lack of appreciation for the science underpinning it, that one finds it difficult to change the outlook of not only laymen but also many bureaucrats on this point.

17. *A Pattern in Giving the Nobel Prize*

Every year during October, I eagerly await the announcement of the winners of the Nobel Prizes. The prizes given for science are of particular interest not because the prizes in the other fields carry less value or prestige but because one cannot escape the feeling that those awards may have been slightly influenced by extraneous factors like political considerations or the exaggerated importance attached to any one aspect, leaving scope for faulty judgement. I am therefore confining myself to discussing the science prizes.

A glance at the distribution of the prizes for the year 2000 reveals a pattern that has been perceived in the last few years. America has again got the lion's share. Within America the shift in concentration of prize winners on California, has demolished the so called 'Ivy-League' myth. Barring Harward, the Ivy League group has had no success in recent years. This shows that California is no longer just known for its freeways movies, theme parks, beaches and golden girls. The Ivy League did have an edge at a time when California was concentrating on comparatively trivial matters while the former was devoting itself to the pursuit of intellectual excellence after the model of British universities like Cambridge and Oxford, which by the way can still boast of men of calibre like Stephen Hawking and Roger Penrose whose genius cannot be measured in terms of a Nobel Prize.

Let us look at the prizes given in the year 2000. Ours is an age of information. Information technology is the 'catch phrase' which college students, corporate executives and civil servants liberally use. Not since the time of Claude Shannan, the father of 'information theory', has there been the kind of growth in that field as we are now witnessing. It is in this context that we must view the awards for physics in a world whose skies are crowded with satellite messages and cellular phone traffic. The Nobel committee awarded half of the prize to Jack Kibly of Texas Instruments for his work in developing integrated circuits and as co-inventor of the pocket calculator. (It was Kibly who had the foresight to switch over to Silicon from Geranium to suit the special requirements of transistors.) In a sense Kibly is regarded as the father of the microchip. The other half of the prize went jointly to

Herbert Kroener of the University of California at Santa Barbara and Russia's Zhores Alferov for their fundamental work leading to the creation of every day marvels such as cellular phones and pocket calculators.

The chemistry prize was shared by Hideki Shirekawa of Japan, who accidentally created a kind of polyacytelene and who while working with Ala Heegan of the University of California at Santa Barbara and Alan MacDiarmid of Pennsylvania doped the new material with iodine leading to the creation of conductive plastic, making plastic a miracle conductor.

The focus in respect of prizes for medicine has shifted to neurophysiology. Carlsson's (Sweden) discovery that the lack of the neurotransmitter dopamine causes Parkinson's disease, Greengard's (New York University) explanation as to how dopamine and other neurotransmitters act on the nervous system and the Austrian born Eric Kandel's (Columbia) work which throws light on how the efficiency of synapses in the brain can be modified have won recognition.

Thus the millennium begins with the Nobel committee rewarding imaginative innovators in advanced technology (in both physics and chemistry) who have improved the quality of life by creating fantastic and radically new kinds of devices. In the medical field they have recognized research that has led to alleviating human suffering caused by hitherto little understood diseases affecting the brain.

But the committee's rationalization for still not recognizing the work of Stephen Hawking, widely regarded as Einstein's successor, as they are not sure that his work applies to nature, has perhaps no justification in as much as many would consider Hawking as the finest product of evolution and therefore represents nature itself!

While the exclusion of Hawking does not exactly enhance the image of the Nobel committee, his inclusion would have added lustre to the medal.

18. *Modern Times*

Long before the advent of modern cinematographic techniques involving the use of complex visual and audio effects, three of the greatest comedians in movie history, Charlie Chaplin and Laurel and Hardy in two different movies demonstrated the absurd lengths to which modernization can go.

In the first one Charlie Chaplin as a worker, in an assembly line in an automated factory, goes through an ordeal of impossible contortions and manoeuvres to parody the effects of automation. At one stage he finds himself sandwiched between two layers of a huge machine, and is totally under the control of a conveyor belt moving back and forth in whichever direction he is pushed. At last he emerges totally dazed. At the end of the day when he staggers out of the factory his hands and fingers continue to keep screwing and tightening imaginary nuts and bolts mechanically.

Even more hilarious is the scene in which he is strapped to a chain and fed all kinds of food. The automatic machine suddenly goes haywire throwing the entire process out of gear. Parts of the machinery become erratic, delivering mechanical shocks to his head and teeth. Good old Charlie gives his verdict on types of automation that are counter-productive.

In another movie, Laurel and Hardy enact a sequence in which they sit for dinner with an eccentric inventor. Being hungry they conjure up visions of juicy steaks, and delicious ice-creams. What they get on their plates, instead, are pills of various colours and sizes. Apparently their eccentric host had reduced human requirement of all nutrients to the size of small pills. Thus one pill supplied protein, another vitamins and yet another carbohydrate. In this hilarious sequence the two great comedians show that life is not mere arithmetic involving subtraction or addition but is meant to be lived in the real sense to its fullest potential giving an opportunity to all our senses to interact with the environment.

It is for this reason that the thought of the fully automated home of the future frightens us, though ironically some people take pride in it. They tell us that in future we do not have to go to a shop or a Mall for anything being sold there can be brought to you. All the commodities will be classified and coded and computerized. Suppose you have to buy a shirt of a certain size and colour, all you have to do is to press a button in the home computer. The supermarket will deliver it with speed through a special pipeline, deducting the appropriate money from your account.

A friend of mine who lives in America expressed his sympathy for me when I said that I was going to a book store to buy a book, pointing out that he could order any book in the world through the internet. Of course there was no point in educating him about the pleasure of looking for a book in a real bookshop, browsing through its contents and then making the purchase. No wonder I did not find a single book on his shelf at his house.

This is an age of computers. From corporate executives to travel-agents, scientists to students, everyone is using the computer for some purpose. No doubt the computer has made life easy, since it can do hundreds of things at lightning speed. No one can afford to be computer illiterate in this era of speed and precision, when complex calculations have to be performed in a very short time. But mere admiration for a computer without a corresponding appreciation of the revolutions in electrical engineering and electronics will not give anyone, let alone a student, an opportunity to look at the computer in its proper perspective. How can we pardon a student who enthusiastically talks about his personal computer but is ignorant of the work of early pioneers like Kirchoff, Tesla, Ohm, Oersted, Ampere and Gausse.

Visitors to England's Oxford University, perhaps the greatest name in all education, are politely cautioned against the use of computers inside the university as a matter of principle. They are welcome to use it elsewhere. The moral behind the guideline is not that the computer should be shunned as a gadget but that good traditions must not be lost sight of in our over-enthusiasm for modern devices—an example of Oxonion snobbery coupled with British humour.

Information technology to here is stay and the coming years are going to witness the development of incredibly mind boggling devices such as we had never imagined. But how can we forget that the highway leading to such a sophisticated technology did not start by itself from nowhere. It had its origins in the firm and solid foundations laid by some of the giants of physics, e.g. Faraday's experiments and Maxwell's electro-magnetic theory.

The next time you hear someone dropping computer jargon like access, download, scan and log-in you would be justified in displaying a patronizing grin suggesting that all this would never have come about without the basic advances in electrical technology and electronics, a factor no one seems to realize.

19. *By Word*

To err is human, but to really foul things up requires a computer.

Farmer's Almanac, 1978

A friend of mine who lives abroad and who is of the view that I am wasting far too much time and energy in writing my articles by hand instead of using a word processor gave two seemingly convincing reasons to shed what he regards as my rather old-fashioned practice. With great enthusiasm and an air of finality he declared that the word processor would enable me to check and rectify spelling and grammatical mistakes, assist me in choosing the appropriate word to make a sentence more attractive, arrange the sequence of sentences within a paragraph and even organize the paragraphs in the entire essay, so that the final product turns out to be a flawless gem of superb prose which my tired fingers and my Uniball pen would never hope to achieve.

This sermon naturally set me thinking as to whether I should alter my entire approach to the task of writing articles so as to not only make my work easier but also be in tune with the modern environment of the scientific art of essay writing.

Anyway, before switching to the 'computer option', I thought it would be wise to ascertain the opinion of a renowned scientist whose views I respect and whose range of interests covers a wide spectrum that includes science, history, art, literature and even current affairs. I felt that his perception would be free from any bias. He felt there was no need for me to switch over to a computer.

I must admit that I also appreciate the benefits we have derived from the computer. There is hardly any aspect of life that has not felt the impact of computers. Satellites and surgical procedures, medical investigation and manufacture of synthetic drugs, complicated calculations, communications, cellphones and digital cameras have revolutionized our living conditions.

Why, then, did the scientist tell me that there was no need to switch over to a word processor for the purpose of generating my articles? This viewpoint, incidentally, happens to coincide with my own. His views are best illustrated by the following surprisingly simple, yet compellingly, convincing argument. Let us assume, for example, that I type 'I heat hypocrites' instead of 'I hate hypocrites'. The computer will raise no objection, because the words 'heat' and 'hate' are both found in its own dictionary. But if I were to type out 'I heet hypocrites', the computer will highlight (reject) 'heet' since that word is not to be found in its dictionary!

No doubt the computer is useful in pointing out errors that creep in due to carelessness. Its twin programmes, Spellcheck and Grammatik, will unfailingly point out any spelling mistakes, though the British words 'colour' and 'programme' will not for obvious reasons, be accepted by Spellcheck if their American equivalents 'color' and 'program' alone are found in the dictionary. Shakespeare's great quotation from *Macbeth* 'Tomorrow and tomorrow and tomorrow', will be 'highlighted' by Grammatik as a sentence containing repetitive words, not to mention the famous fourfold negative, 'No, no, no, no' from *King Lear* which only the great Lawrence Olivier could deliver in a rising crescendo to bring out the full agony felt by the king.

By the same token 'put out the light, and then put out the light' from *Othello* will also be rejected. Nor can our 'wonder machine' even comprehend the famous quotation from *Macbeth*, 'If it were done when 'tis done then 'twere well it were done quickly'.

Put briefly, our 'technological marvel' is good for correcting spelling mistakes in communications of a routine nature particularly if the level of vocabulary is not very high. But when confronted with the lyrical tidal wave of a Shakespearean soliloquy or the literary grandeur of Miltonic verse, it is struck dumb. Of course, I have not taken into consideration the ability of an infant to recognize its mother's face even when turned by ninety degrees, which a computer cannot do, unless specifically programmed to do so.

To end the discussion on a lighter vein I would like to draw attention to an apocryphal anecdote about a man who applied to a computerized marriage bureau listing out the features he wanted in his life partner: 'Cute, dignified, of good stature and gait, very friendly, a good listener and someone willing to be cuddled and fondled all the time without complaining of a headache.' The bureau suggested a penguin!

20. *A New Dimension: Was Einstein Wrong?*

Having regard to the reputation of *Nature* as the most prestigious scientific journal in the world, one cannot brush aside the discovery of Paul Davies that light might have been travelling at 'infinite speed' at the point of creation of the universe and has slowed down to the present uniform velocity of 3,00,000 km/sec throughout the Universe.

As Davies himself has observed in one of his books this velocity of 3,00,000 km/sec in vacuum is the limiting speed of any subatomic particle. It is known that water slows down light to 2,30,000 km/sec. This would imply that a light speed subatomic particle travelling at 3,00,000 km/sec through water would travel actually faster than light travels in water producing and 'electromagnetic shock' called the 'Cerenkov Radiation' (named after its discoverer) just as an aircraft travelling faster than sound would produce a sonic boom.

In this context we have to necessarily make a mention about the history of measurement of velocity of light. Based on a study of eclipses, a Danish astronomer O.L. Romer had suggested in the seventeenth century that it was possible to calculate the velocity of light. (If some modern numbers are used it works out to 300,000 km/sec.) Again in 1851, French physicist Jean Foucault had for the first time calculated the speed of light in a laboratory up to an accuracy of 2,80,000 km/sec besides suggesting that it would be reduced in water. Another physicist Fresnel also had come to similar conclusions independently.

Then in 1905, Einstein turned upside down all classical notions about physics. He was faced with the problem of how to reconcile the theory of relativity with the behaviour of light and other electromagnetic phenomena particularly when he was adamant that his exotic new theory of relativity must be upheld at any cost. On the one hand there was the theory of the Austrian scientist Ernst Mach (known for giving his name to the speed of sound) who had held that all motion had to be 'relative'. On the other hand, Einstein was totally against rejecting the theory of electrodynamics with its unique value for the velocity of light. In one magnificent leap of intellect, Einstein retained the relativity of uniform motion and the constancy of the speed of light as the founding principles of his new theory of relativity. In order to do this, he gave up the universality of time space a compromise or more accurately a 'reconciliation'.

But there are some erroneous notions about the theory of relativity such as that it is impossible in principle for something to travel faster than light. On the other hand as astronomer John Gribbin has observed all that relativity says is that it is not possible to cross the speed of light 'barrier'. This would mean that if a particle is travelling slower than light, it would take an infinite amount of energy even to accelerate it up to the speed of light. In other words if a particle did exist that travelled faster than light it would always travel faster than light. This means that on the either side of the light barrier it would require an infinite amount of energy to slow it down to light speed. Einstein's equation do allow for the possible existence of 'faster than light' particles, 'Tachyons' from the Greek word 'swift' as they are called (many scientists have speculated about the existence of the Tachyon, including experimental physicist Roger Clay of Austria in 1974 and India's George Sudarshan, who was director of MAT science. But no Tachyon have yet been isolated or detected) as compared to the patronizing same of 'Tardons' given to slower than light particles by some physicists. The light barrier is then some kind of a 'threshold' which is, impenetrable—and creates a kind of paradox; particles 'slower than light' *i.e.* on our side of a 'hypothetical ridge' get slower as they roll down unless given an energy boost, while particles on the other side of the ridge, roll down to higher speeds, unless they are also given an energy boost. Time runs more and more slowly as you approach the speed of light, climbing the ridge from our side and coming to a halt at the light speed. But the same token, time should run backwards slowly on the other side and even more backwards for tachyons, moving more and more rapidly as they descend the ridge on the other side, moving away from the speed of light. This has been graphically described by John Gribbin.

If this is so, it may account for the findings of Paul Davies that light had infinite speed at the point of creation and gradually slowed down stopping at the barrier of 3,00,000 km/sec (the present velocity).

It is, therefore, incorrect to say Davies has turned the theories of Einstein upside down. It would be perhaps more appropriate to regard the findings of Davies as an improvement or refinement of a certain aspect of Relativity. In science, old theories constantly get 'modified' with later developments. Many concepts are likely to remain unchanged or undergo slight modifications. The technological benefits arising out of Relativity cannot be obliterated by the modification of many of its principles.

Therefore, even if Davies has made a breakthrough by way of a major modification of Einstein's theory of the Velocity of Light, which may compel us to revise several concepts in various areas, we still cannot afford to brush aside the immense technological benefits that were derived from the implications of Relativity—the principles on which such a powerful tool as the Electron Microscope is based, the principle that led to the making of the Klystron electron tubes that supply microwave power to radars. Of course the best indication of the correctness of Relativity is the huge particle accelerators that accelerate sub atomic particles like electrons and protons to the velocity of light and the enormous energy that can be derived from the atom and used for peaceful purpose if not for destruction.

The disclosure of Davies comes just at a time when physics has entered a crucial state in its entire history. To sum up, let us take Davies seriously and not as one of those senile characters who claim from time to time about having disproved relativity or rediscovered it. But it will take quite a while for the implications of the findings of Davies to be fully realized in the context of the validity of a theory that has been regarded as one of the three greatest triumphs of science in the twentieth century—the other two being—Quantum Mechanics and the elucidation of the structure of the DNA (Deoxyribonucleic acid).

21. *A Pseudo-science of the Sky*

If Homeopathy and Vaasthu are regarded as pseudo-sciences on earth then astrology, the third pseudo-science literally hits the sky.

At the outset, let us take one of the hallmarks of Astrology, its facile discrimination in dividing humanity into twelve groups with no basis or justification, corresponding to the twelve signs of the so-called Zodiac. Indeed this becomes the main topic of discussion in almost all social gatherings, parties and friendly discussions. The conversation may start in a light-hearted manner but soon tempers come into play as allegations and counter-allegations are levelled, ending sometimes in violence. Even advertisements in newspapers seeking partners for marriage explicitly indicate good horoscopes.

Astrologers talk with gusto about Aquarius moving into Saturn or Leo moving into Neptune while attempting to make predictions. Saturn and Neptune being planets are real entities but Aquarius and Leo being clusters of stars are not. Hence the question of a cluster of stars moving into a planet not only does not arise, but constitutes the height of absurdity. And even more nonsensical is the suggestion that someone's moon or Jupiter is influenced by Taurus or Libra.

As eminent evolutionary biologist Richard Dawkins points out nobody has ever produced any evidence that the movements of planets with respect to constellations actually have the slightest influence on human affairs. There is no physical law whereby the position of distant stellar bodies at the moment of your birth could exert any casual influence on your life. Scientific studies on astrology have yielded no positive results. Such isolated cases where some sort of weak correlation between star sign and character was noticed have a simple explanation. Devotees of astrology know what traits are expected of them and accordingly live up to the expectations not to a significant degree but enough to make claims in a drawing room. The domineering Leo wife may dismiss her Aquarian husband as an imaginative dreamer since that is what astrology says.

There is a test known as reliability. It is to see whether different practitioners (astrologers in this case) when confronted with the same evidence (or the same astrologer confronted with the same evidence twice) agree. Alas they don't.

Despite the fact that all over the world books on astrology outsell astronomy, let us be clear that astronomy is the only science that is qualified to study heavenly bodies. Its offshoot, astro-physics, also has naturally the same sanctity. Everything we know about the universe today, including the solar system, its birth, evolution and fate is the result of hundreds of years of fruitful research in these two pure sciences. Any other exercise based on conjecture, guess work, super stition and assumptions would amount to a fraud. This kind of ignorance can perhaps be forgiven if we are dealing with a primitive society or before the advent of modern science. But at this stage in the evolution of human society, to talk about stellar objects influencing human destiny is unforgivable in engineers and doctors, let alone bureaucrats politicians and business executives.

First let us have look at a constellation. Richard Dawkins convincingly argues that a constellation is a miscellaneous cluster of stars all being billions and billions of miles from each other. The stars are unconnected with each other except that they seem to have a certain shape or pattern when seen from the earth. Since there is no real line connecting the stars the patterns perceived are imaginary. Hence one cluster may look like a lion, another like a bull and a third like a fish. Stars are also constantly on the move and the shape or pattern of a constellation is ephemeral. Homo erectus looked at a set of very different constellations a million year ago. A million years later our descendants would see constellations of different shapes. Astronomers can predict what those shapes will look like whereas astrologers do not have any clue !

Yet another aspect about human nature itself is that people remember correct guesses but ignore wrong predictions. People are so impressed with an accurate guess (by sheer coincidence) that they gloss over the rest of the comments. There are also safe bets like foreign travel in the offing if you 'play your cards right' or 'be cautious about what you eat on Wednesday as you may fall sick' or 'be calm while talking to your spouse on Friday as domestic harmony may be disrupted'. These are remarks which shake the very foundations of astrology for if an event is preordained how can you prevent it by taking precautions.

This most unscientific discipline then has gained popularity by exploiting the gullible, the ignorant and the superstitious. One wonders why professional astrologers are not being prosecuted for fraud when manufacturers making false claims for their products are being prosecuted.

Let us therefore march forward in this great scientific age of information technology, discarding astrology into the dustbin of history. Otherwise posterity will never forgive us. At this stage it is only appropriate to recall the lines of the greatest genius mankind has ever produced: 'that men and not the influence of stars determine their own destiny'.

> The fault dear Brutus is not in our stars,
> But in ourselves, that we are underlings.

SHAKESPEARE in *Julius Ceasar*

PART II

MEDICAL SCIENCE

22. *Abandonment*

Nor bring, to see me cease to live,
Some doctors full of phrase and fame,
To shake his sapient head and give
The ill he cannot cure a name.

MATHEW ARNOLD

Medical Treatment is based on the ethical principle that nothing should be more important to a doctor than the 'best interests' of the patient he is trying to cure. This is particularly relevant in respect of diseases like cancer where a combination of measures like surgery, radiation and clinical therapy results in agony or debility. (Of course, if the type of cancer is potentially remediable one cannot avoid trying out such options even if they are painful.)

A person decides to become a doctor.

(a) for the sake of having a decent job, or
(b) because he has a special aptitude for becoming a practitioner, or
(c) because it is a very lucrative profession.

The order in which these criteria have been listed is no reflection of their relative importance. Any two or all three of the above may provide the necessary motivation in any particular individual. However, more than all these is the 'satisfaction' that the very nature of the work provides—the light of gratitude in a sick patient's eyes.

For is there anything to rival the hope that a physician's mere presence in the room of a sick person brings to a worried family? The simple piece of information that the doctor is on his way dramatically alters the atmosphere in a house from helpless terror to a sense of security that somehow the crisis will be overcome. There is something about the angel who walks into a house with a smile and confidence and whose very entrance into the patient's room reassures everyone, that touches the hem of divinity.

The aim of every doctor is to correctly diagnose a patient's illness and effect a cure. (Every doctor takes this as a 'challenge' and employs the entire arsenal at his command, the instruments with which he measures all the physiological parameters related to the sick person and compares them with the 'constants' to arrive at a diagnosis. The more complicated the disease is the greater the 'challenge', a factor that motivates the doctor to constantly improve his clinical ability. But often the process of improving his skills leads the doctor to a 'paradoxical situation' where the emphasis shifts from 'curing the patient' to 'overcoming the challenge'.

Dealing with the 'challenge' becomes an 'end' in itself, and even in situations where the doctor finds himself losing the battle with the disease and the chances of success seem remote, the addiction to try out every option is too strong for him to give up the struggle.

At the same time, the patient having developed a psychological dependence on the doctor not only believes implicitly in his competence, but also accepts any suggestion made by the doctor partly in the belief that he must have some genuine reason and partly out of his fear of offending him. All the sophisticated instruments and the electronic gadgets in the intensive care unit, represent to the dying man the determination of his doctor not to yield, whereas to the doctor himself, the technical panoply and the dying person only represent the test of his efficiency. If he fails, it is a blow to his self-esteem and a sign of weakness and impotence. The only course open for him is to disappear emotionally as well as 'physically'—a phenomenon known as 'abandonment' of the patient by the doctor.

Now why does this happen? As long as a doctor has even the slightest hope of saving a dying man, he has the zeal to try out every weapon in his armoury. He is the visible symbol of strength and the power of modern medicine. The moment he becomes certain that he is fighting a losing battle he is reluctant to admit defeat and face a situation where his own power and skill and the triumphs of modern medical technology are useless against the forces of nature. The challenge no longer exists and his power has no meaning. His inability to face the consequences leaves him with no option but to disappear unobtrusively. He is afraid of Heaven making him

> A fixed figure for the time of scorn
> And point his slow unmoving finger at.

as Othello said in Shakespeare's immortal lines.

The hope of overcoming the challenge against all odds created by this hi-tech, bio-medical era turns out to be an illusion and a deception. It is better to call it a day at a much earlier stage, giving the confused patient enough time to attend to 'intensely private and unfinished matters' relating to conflicts, relationships and business. For in the absence of false hopes he can have one 'longing lingering look' at life and a chance to say in the immortal words of Robert Frost:

> I have promises to keep
> And miles to go before I sleep.

23. *Peace in the Face of Death: Endorphins Calm the Nerves*

Cowards die many times before their deaths;
The valiant never taste of death but once
Of all the wonders that I yet have heard
It seems to me most strange that men should fear:
Seeing that death a necessary end,
Will come when it will come.

SHAKESPEARE

Shakespeare makes Julius Caesar say these words to Calpurnia before leaving for the Senate when she expresses fear for his safety. However with the exception of a handful, people have dreaded death since the dawn of history. Thrust into this 'bank and shoal of time without choice or awareness from an unknown void as an infant, the fear of death, that undiscovered country from whose bourn no traveller returns' makes man bear the ills rather than fly to others he knows not of. However, of all forms of life on earth, man alone is fortunate in possessing in abundance two remarkable faculties, intelligence and imagination, which have enabled him to manipulate the environment for his own benefit.

While his intelligence has led him to unearth the secrets of nature and invent marvellous devices that have revolutionized his quality of life, imagination makes him the only creature which can plan and enjoy any kind of experience.

But unfortunately man's very strength is his greatest weakness. The constant awareness that his life-span is limited and is always in the danger of being terminated abruptly casts a pall of gloom over his existence. This brings us to one of the greatest puzzles in medical science as to how mortally wounded soldiers experience no fear or panic, and continue to fight till death, how young children despite being fatally stabbed by psychopaths show no sign of fear or agony on their faces, but only tranquillity and peace before they die. Medical history is replete with such accounts.

In 1844 the great explorer Livingstone had been trying to protect some natives from a lion when it seized him by his arm. The lion was shot dead but not before it had inflicted grave injuries. Livingstone had been shaken by the lion's jaws, like a mouse by a cat, but he had only felt a sort of dreaminess and euphoria—not terror or pain. Similarly Montaigne, when pushed down from a horse and anticipating his death, experienced no fear or panic but only tranquillity and it was only much later that he felt any kind of pain. Patients undergoing surgery feel pain when the effect of anaesthesia wears off.

It is, therefore, possible that just when a person is in danger of imminent death, the body itself produces an 'opiate like' substance that acts like an anaesthetic—appropriately named Endorphin. Endon in Greek means 'within', gennao means 'I produce'; and Morpheus is the Roman God of Sleep and Dreams. Thus endogenous morphines have given rise to the word 'Endorphin'.

In response to stress, Endorphins originate in the hypothalamus and pituitary glands and an area called the periaqueductal gray matter, and along with ACTH—a hormone that activates the adrenal gland, bind themselves onto receptors on the surface of certain nerve cells. They raise the pain threshold and act only when there is 'trauma', not otherwise.

There is reason to believe that the same process is at work in the case of acupuncture. It would seem that vibrating or rotating needles at some specific points on the human body stimulates the secretion and outpouring of endorphins. How else can one explains complicated surgical procedures being performed without anaesthesia in many parts of China?

A rise in the levels of endorphins has actually been documented not only in certain medical institutions in China but also in some laboratories in the West. However the precise neurological route by which signals travel and stimulate the brain to produce endorphins has not yet been identified.

There is as yet no explanation for this phenomenon but these substances (endorphin) seem to have evolved as a physiological survival mechanism to protect mammals and other animals from terror and pain during the earth's early history when threatening events had been occurring frequently due to predators or natural calamities.

While our knowledge of endorphins is still in its infancy, there is credible speculation that, in some mysterious manner, factors such as these seem to be at work (not just the rush of adrenaline) introducing calmness and equanimity in the last stages of patients suffering from terminal illness, so as to not only make them accept the inevitable end but, also in some cases invite death.

As only Keats could have said:

> I have been half in love with easeful death
> Call'd him soft names in many a mused rhyme
> To take into the air my quiet breath;
> Now more than ever seems it rich to die
> To cease upon the midnight with no pain.

24. *Obsessive Compulsive Disorder: Strange Obsessions that Throttle Life*

> Anguish of mind has driven thousands to suicide; anguish of body, none. This proves that the health of the mind is of far more consequence to our happiness than the health of the body, although both are deserving of much more attention than either of them receives.
>
> COLTON

It is one of the strangest ironies of modern medical practice that when science is armed to the teeth to fight some of the greatest scourges such as cancer and AIDS, a seemingly simple mental disorder which is widely prevalent all over the world has stubbornly continued to defy medical treatment. Known as 'obsessive compulsive disorder' (OCD), the malady is a manifestation of a general category of mental disorders knows as anxiety neuroses.

One famous psychologist, when asked to spell out the difference between psychosis and neurosis, observed that while a phychotic has absolutely no insight at all into his mental condition, a neurotic is aware of the problem agitating his mind. For example, a psychotic would confidently declare to society and friends that he is Napoleon. No attempt to convince him that he is not the famous French General would be successful. As such, the psychotic really does not suffer any mental agony as long as the delusion does not get out of hand and land him and society in serious trouble. The neurotic, on the other hand, would be agitated by the obsessive thought that he is Napoleon while he himself knows very well that he is someone else.

What distinguishes the two, however, is that in the case of the neurotic, his obsessive preoccupation with this nagging thought that he is Napoleon does not allow him to lead a normal life. We need not go into a detailed discussion on the distinction between psychosis and neurosis because there are several kinds of psychoses in which the patient suffers mental agony, e.g. kinds of schizophrenia like for example, those of the persecutory kind where the patient claims to be hearing voices and constantly apprehends threats to his life from imaginary enemies.

Quality of life

Leaving aside such serious forms of psychoses, one would be justified in concluding that generally speaking it is the neurotic who suffers more in day-to-day life. On the one hand his mental condition may not warrant confinement in a mental asylum on the other his obsessions and compulsions torment him. In addition, the quality of life is severely diminished depriving him of precious years of productive existence.

What is particularly painful is that obsessive compulsive disorder is widely prevalent and it may be found in addition to the normal physical ailments brought by the average patient to the notice of a physician or a surgeon. In such cases, the surgeon treats the physical ailment in isolation and totally ignores the mental aspect. Since the emphasis of therapy is on the physical ailment, the mental component goes totally unnoticed. This is perhaps because the average doctor has neither time nor sympathy for a patient who adds a mental twist to his ailment. At the most the physician may prescribe a tranquillizer in the hope it would reduce the anxiety. Physicians grievously err in underestimating the impact of the mental factor on the general health of the patient. Given below are a few samples where the symptoms of the disorder are manifest in the behaviour pattern of many individuals.

Let us take the case of Rao. If you met Rao at a party or business meeting, you would think he is a pretty ordinary person. He might tell you he works as an executive, that he is married but has no children, and that he likes watching sporting events on television. You probably wouldn't notice that he refuses to eat any food offered to him at the party, and that he quietly disappears to the bathroom five times in the course of only a few hours. His hands are red, raw and blistered. Rao suffers from a compulsion to wash his hands as many as 40 times a day since he was 16 years old. Any time he thinks his hands might be dirty, say from touching a piece of food, taking out the garbage, or dusting his apartment, he immediately gets an irresistible urge to wash them. He knows that this kind of dirt is not dangerous and that his hand washing is completely excessive.

For entirely mysterious reasons, however, the urge to wash his hands is overwhelming: if he doesn't do it he feels an intolerable anxiety. Once he washes, he immediately relaxes, until the next time. He can't travel or sit in a movie theatre long because he has to know that a sink and soap are nearby. Some times he gets so sick of his compulsion that he becomes extremely depressed. No matter how hard he tries, he cannot stop washing his hands.

Different compulsions

Rao has classic compulsions as part of his obsessive-compulsive disorder. Like many patients he has had symptoms from adolescence—some people get this as young children—and he is tortured by the compulsions. He does not really want to wash his hands, but he cannot stop. Other patients have different compulsions, for example, the fastidious housewife who keeps scrubbing the floors over and over to be sure there is no dirt, checking more than a hundred times that the gas stove is turned off before leaving home.

Another example is Vijayalakshmi, who works in a travel agency. She does fairly good work and has a compulsive urge to impress everyone. This puzzles her bosses because they think she is unusually intelligent, dedicated and there is no need for her to advertise her efficiency. Yet, she cannot resist the temptation to do so. The reason is that the main motivating force behind her work is the compulsion to impress everyone, particularly her boss. Vijayalakshmi spends most of her time ruminating as to whether her efficiency has been noticed and as to how many clients have been captivated by her charm.

Like Rao, Vijayalakshmi hasn't the slightest idea why she needs to impress everyone or why she is obsessively concerned as to whether she has created a good impact on people. These obsessive doubts can be disturbing, when she feels that she has displeased the boss. At night she may remain awake trying to remember what action of hers annoyed the boss. She has a combination of compulsions—needing to perform and impress—and obsessions haunting her mind about the mistakes she thinks she has committed. No one is aware of her behaviour and the bosses simply think she is fussy. Vijayalakshmi is not married and nor has established a long-term healthy relationship with anyone. She would do anything to stop her compulsions and obsessions, but no amount of effort works. Her obsessive compulsive urge to impress her boss by her hardwork and success at public relations continues to torment her.

Take the case of Bharati who appears normal. She is married, has two kids and goes to work. But, deep inside she feels like a mess. Her husband is ready to abandon her and the children are often withdrawn and upset. She is distant from her family and locked in the hell of an obsessive compulsive disorder. She cleans her house for hours every night after work. She screams at her husband and children when anything is out of place. She washes her hands often and asks her husband and kids to do the same.

Unwanted thoughts

Obsessive compulsive disorder is thus characterized by obsessions and compulsions that are usually chronic. Obsessions refer to recurrent and unwanted thoughts that cause anxiety and discomfort because of their aggressive, sexual or disgusting content. Compulsions are apparent in behaviour like hand-washing and checking the stove or door lock.

OCD should not be confused with a compulsive personality. An OCD patient suffers from a compulsion that must be resisted whereas a compulsive personality disorder patient is happy in his orderliness or stinginess. To determine if you have OCD, ask yourself whether you have repetitive thoughts that seem horrible or weird or if there are things you do over and over again.

A survey conducted a few years ago in the United States found that OCD was 50-100 times more common than previously believed, affecting 1 to 2 per cent of the population worldwide, and making it the fourth most common psychiatric disorder (after phobias, substance abuse, and major depression). There are two problems with this finding. One being that it was based on reports made by lay interviewers, and it included no careful evaluation of how the symptoms impaired the OCD sufferers. However, other studies have addressed these shortcomings and found OCD to be as common as the survey showed. Patients with OCD are also more likely to have schizophrenia, depression, Tourette's syndrome (involuntary muscle tics and vocal tics, including absence words) and other anxiety disorders.

Formerly thought to be a rare condition, OCD now affects as many as a million people in the United States alone. The figures in our country must be even larger. This disorder, almost without expectation, dramatically impairs a person's functioning and often affects the whole family. OCD is often noticed first by outside people.

Hallmarks

The hallmarks of this disorder are obsession (recurrent disgusting or frightening thoughts) or compulsions (behaviour that a person knows make no sense but feels compelled to do any way) the obsessive thoughts are usually senseless and repugnant. They may involve repetitive thoughts of violence (such as killing one's child), contamination (such as becoming infected by shaking hands), or doubts (such as having hurt someone in a road accident even though no such accident had occurred). The more a person tries to control them, the stronger becomes their hold over him.

The most common compulsions involve hand-washing, counting, checking and touching. These are often performed according to certain rules in a strict or rigid manner. For example, a person with a counting compulsion may feel the need to count every crack on the pavement on the way to work or school. What would be a five-minute walk could turn out to be a three to four hour's trip. The great English writer Samuel Johnson is said to have suffered from this disorder.

The intensity of OCD varies widely. Some people have milder versions. For instance, they feel that the house should be clean before going on a vacation and start worrying about the condition of the house. More serious forms of this disorder can make a person housebound. A 25 year old girl who had obsessive sexual thoughts made her feel dirty inside. It reached the point where she would lock all the doors, draw the shades, turn off the lights, so as to make a futile attempt to shut out the abhorrent sexual thoughts as they came into her mind. Eventually normal life became impossible and she had to be hospitalized.

People with these disorders get stuck on unwanted, repetitive thoughts and cannot banish them from their minds unless they act in a specific manner. Some bizarre versions of this condition are trichotillomania (plucking one's own hair), onychophagia (nail biting), Tourette's syndrome, hypochondria, autism, compulsive shopping, pathological gambling, chronic pain, addictive disorders, eating disorders and oppositional defiant disorder.

Note: The names Rao, Vijayalakshmi and Bharati are fictitious. Any resemblance to real or dead persons in a mere coincidence and not intended to cause embarrassment.

25. *Obsessive Compulsive Disorder: Strange Manners Still Fox Researchers*

> It is with diseases of the mind as with diseases of the body, we are half dead before we understand our disorder, and half cured when we do.
>
> COLTON

How does one treat a patient who suffers from complications associated with obsessive compulsive disorder (OCD). This article throws light on some latest therapeutic method.

There are behavioural psychotherapies that may work for some patients with OCD, but this is a very hard condition to treat. Almost all patients ultimately take some medication in addition to therapy.

No single treatment seems completely beneficial for this condition, not even long-term psychotherapy, behavioural psychotherapy or drug therapy. However, OCD has recently become the subject of intense scientific study and some good treatments are beginning to emerge. Consequently, the situation is substantially brighter now.

There are many psychological theories about the cause of this serious illness, but it is agreed that it is one of the most biological of all mental disorders. Patients with OCD may seem perfectly normal to the casual observer. They often have none of the odd behaviour or strange mannerisms common to some psychotic or schizophrenic patients. But the obsessive compulsive patient is a prisoner to senseless thoughts and the need to repeat meaningless rituals. Sometimes he may become very depressed over his behaviour, though it is rare for patients with OCD to attempt suicide. The patient doesn't actually believe his hands are so dirty as to warrant incessant washing. He often swears he will stop. But he cannot. Something—a brain abnormality, perhaps—forces him to have the obsessions and act out the compulsions over and over.

Psychiatric drugs and OCD

Almost every psychiatric drug known has been used to treat OCD, including Tricyclic antidepressants, SSRI antidepressants, MAIOs

(Monoamine Oxidase Inhibitor), antipsychotic drugs, amphetamines, clonidine, and tranquillizers. Electroshock treatment is reported to work sometimes, but these treatments work only in exceptional cases.

Two kinds of drugs are now known to have specific anti-obsessive-compulsive properties: the Tricyclic antidepressant Anafranil and the Selective Serotonin Reuptake Inhibitors (SSRIs) Luvox, Prozac, Paxil and Zoloft. Since the primary FDA approval in the United States was given for Anafranil and Luvox for the treatment of OCD, they are included here. Paxil, Prozac and Zoloft have also been approved for treatment of depression. However, SSRI drugs are often regarded as equally effective. Anafranil may be slightly more effective for OCD than the SSRIs, but also has more side effects.

The brain's billions of nerve cells communicate with each other largely via neurotransmitters. Typically, a nerve cell, or neuron, will manufacture a neurotransmitter and then excrete it into the gap, or synapse, between it and an adjoining nerve cell. When the neurotransmitter makes contact with a receptor on the surface of the second nerve cell, the 'message' or nerve impulse is then transmitted from one nerve cell to the next. Millions of such messages are sent every second in the human brain.

So far, several dozen of these chemical messengers, or neurotransmitters, have been identified. Several of these neurotransmitters—norepinephrine, dopamine and serotonin—seem to play major roles in governing a person's mood, and all the antidepressants (the MAOIs, tricyclics and SSRIs) work by boosting brain levels of one or more of the chemical.

Serotonin: A ray of hope

Among the mood-affecting neurotransmitters, serotonin seems to be especially important. It's the primary neurotransmitter that drug designers have targeted over the past 10 years in trying to synthesize antidepressant drugs—an effort that has led to the development of prozac and the other SSRIs now in the market.

All the SSRIs are based on the principle that depression often results from abnormally low levels of serotonin in the gaps, or synapses, between the nerve cells. The SSRIs boost synoptic levels of serotonin, and the increase serves to rev up communication among nerve cells and eventually results in improved mood.

The SSRIs increase serotonin levels between the cells by capitalizing on the fact that the nerve cells, or neurons, are frugal when it comes to their neurotransmitters and do their best to recycle them. Shortly after neuron A communicates with adjacent neuron B by releasing a dose of serotonin molecules into the synapse between the two cells, neuron A will reabsorb these serotonin molecules through use of special receptors on its surface known as reuptake pumps. Prozac and all the other SSRIs somehow block these pumps so that serotonin cannot be reabsorbed by neuron A. The result: reuptake of serotonin is selectively blocked, serotonin molecules accumulate in the synapses—and depressions are lifted.

Primary treatment

The SSRIs have now become the primary treatment for OCD, along with the tricyclic clomipramine. Serotonin has been studied in OCD and is found to have a role, as it does in aggression, anxiety, learning, social dominance, impulsivity, and suicide. Clomipramine has a potent serotonin effect, and is more effective against OCD than is desipramine, which is a norepinephrine-specific tricyclic. All the SSRIs have proved effective in treating OCD and, combined with behaviour therapy, offer those suffering from this painful and debilitating condition real hope of spending less time obsessively checking, hoarding, and washing, and more time with family, friends, and in meaningful work. This combination therapy helps most people get better, but does not cure them completely. Because OCD is a chronic illness that waxes and wanes, SSRI treatment must be long-term. Symptomatic improvement may continue steadily for months.

In 1991, a scientist in the United States hypothesized that patients with trichotillomania would exhibit the same brain imaging as those with OCD. At rest, these patients exhibited a different brain pattern. Yet when these patients were treated with the antiobsessive antidepressant Anafranil, there was decreased activity in the cingulate region of the frontal lobes, which has also been found with successful treatment of OCD with antiobsessive antidepressants.

Like most forms of psychiatric illness, part of effective treatment for OCD often involves medication. At this writing, there are eight 'antiobsessive medications' and more on the way. The current medications that have shown effectiveness with OCD are Anafranil (clomipramine), Prozac (fluxetine), Zoloft (sertraline), paxil (paroxetine), Effexor (venalafaxine), and Luvox (fluvoxamine). These medicines have provided many patients with profound relief from OCD symptoms.

In addition, behaviour therapy is often helpful. The patient is gradually exposed to situations most likely to bring out the rituals and habits. The therapist teaches the patient thought-stopping techniques and strongly encourages him or her to face his or her worst fear (for example, by persuading a patient with a fear of dirt or contamination to play in the mud).

Hypochondriasis: A tough OCD

However, of all the manifestations of OCD there is perhaps nothing more agonising and difficult to manage than hypochondriasis, or more familiarly, hypochondria, which is a persistent preoccupation with the possibility of having one are more serious progressive physical illnesses such as cancer. Patients show persistent concern with their health, and commonplace sensations such as 'missed' heartbeats generate severe anxiety. Reassurance that there is no underlying organic disease fails to alleviate the condition.

Hypochondriasis may on the surface appear to be merely an annoying manifestation of a nervous temperament. But the patient who has this condition usually suffers the agonies of hell in his own mind. He has an obsessive fear that he is suffering from some form of cancer and on the other, he lacks the courage to go in for investigation, which alone can set his mind at rest. He finds himself in a situation in which he is totally isolated with his own fears. Since his range of suspicion and fear can cover the entire spectrum of the human physiological system, it becomes difficult for the normal physician to constantly keep reassuring him that he has no serious ailment without carrying out a battery of tests for which again the patient is unwilling to subject himself.

Thus, in all medical therapy hypochondriasis is perhaps the single most difficult condition to manage or treat from the point of view of the patient, the members of his family and also the physician, whose task is unenviable. These features are quite common in depressed patients and it can be difficult to determine whether what appears to be hypochondriasis is really a symptom of depression. Hypochondriacal patients have been found to be almost ten times more likely to suffer from a major depression. In some cultures there is a higher tendency to refer to bodily, as distinct from psychological, 'pain'. Hypochondriasis is considered by some to be simply the somatization of depression.

While somatization due to the stigma and shame that can attach to mental illness has been emphasized in non-western societies, its presence in western societies may be grossly under-reported. In one study of 1,000 patients visiting a medical diagnostic clinic, no organic medical illness could be detected in over two-thirds of them. So while physical distress is a main reason for going to a general practitioner, the most common diagnosis is the absence of organic disorder. But one must recognize that it can be very difficult to tell the difference between symptoms that are psychosomatic caused by organic illness. It is important to determine with certainly whether the physical symptoms are concealing a depressive illness or whether they are 'real', that is, due to organic pathology.

It is curious that conversion disorders, made so famous by Freud, in which an emotional conflict was converted into, for example, blindness, deafness or paralysis, seem nowadays to be very rare. One possibility is that many of the cases Freud reported were indeed due to a physical disorder.

A long way to go

Medicine has still a long way to go to help these unfortunate individuals though there has been a radical change of attitude towards their problem. As against the old theories that most mental problems (excluding psychoses) were largely the result of the impact of environmental factors on a person's early life, there is now a realization that the medical changes taking place in the brains of such individuals have to be treated for deficiency or over-activity, as the case may be, by specific drugs such as the SSRIs. In this connection, a part of the brain known as the Cingulate Gyrus has acquired great importance of late.

Thus, for the first time the role of the Cingulate Gyrus and our ability to modulate Serotonin have become front-line weapons in the medical arsenal for overcoming problems such as OCD.

26. *Obsessive Compulsive Disorder: Cingulate Gyrus may Hold the Key*

> A weak mind is like a microscope, which magnifies trifling things, but cannot receive great ones.
>
> CHESTERFIELD

The importance of Serotonin is beginning to be realized as even doctors are seeking nutritional intervention to regulate Serotonin levels.

Traversing longitudinally through the deep central aspects of the frontal lobes is the cingulate gyrus. It's the part of the brain that allows you to shift your attention from one thing to another, to move from one idea to another, to see the options in life. Feelings of safety and security have also been attributed to this part of the brain. Experience has shown that the term that best relates to this part of the brain is Cognitive Flexibility.

Cognitive flexibility defines a person's ability to go with the flow, adapt to change and deal successfully with new problems. Many situations in life demand cognitive flexibility. For example, when you start a new job, you need to learn a new system of doing things. Even if you did something another way at a previous job, learning how to shift to please a new boss or adapt to a new system is critical to job success. Junior high school students need cognitive flexibility in order to be successful in school. In seventh grade, many students begin to get used to having various teachers throughout the day. It is necessary to adapt to the teaching styles of different teachers. Flexibility is also important in friendships. What works in a friendship with one person may not be effective with another.

Effectively managing change and transitions is an essential ingredient in personal, interpersonal and professional growth. The cingulate system can be of great help or hindrance to this process. When it is working properly, we are able to roll along easily with the various developments of the day; when it is impaired or overactive, cognitive flexibility is diminished.

Along with shifting attention, we have seen that cooperation is also influenced by this part of the brain. When the cingulate works effectively it's easy to shift into cooperative modes of behaviour. People with cingulate problems have difficulty in shifting attention and get stuck in ineffective behaviour patterns.

The cingulate system has also been implicated (along with the other aspects of the PFC) in 'future-oriented thinking', such as planning and goal-setting. When this part of the brain works well, it is easier to plan and set reasonable goals. On the negative side, difficulties in this part of the brain can cause a person to perceive fearful situations where there are none, predict negative events and feel unsafe in the world.

Seeing options is crucial to adaptable behaviour. Adaptable physicians readily utilize new ideas and technology (after a scientific basis is developed), and they are open to giving their patients the latest information on what is new and exciting. Physicians who have cingulate problems tend to be rigid, do things the way they have always been done, and be autocratic ('Do it my way if you want me to treat you'). Being able to see options and new ideas protects against stagnation, depression and hostile behaviour.

When the cingulate system is abnormal, people have a tendency to get stuck on things, locked into things, to rethink the same thought over and over. They may become worriers and continually obsess about the same thought. They may hold on to hurts or grudges from the past, unable to let them go. They may also get stuck on negative behaviours or develop compulsions such as hand-washing or excessively checking locks.

One patient who had difficulties in this part of the brain described this phenomenon 'like being on a rat's exercise wheel, where the thoughts just go over and over and over'. Another patient opined: 'It's like having a reset button that is always on. Even though I don't want to have the thought anymore, it just keeps coming back.'

The clinical problems associated with the cingulate will be discussed shortly. There are also a number of 'subclinical patterns' associated with abnormalities in this part of the brain. Subclinical problems are those that don't cause the dysfunction of a full-fledged disorder, but can none the less erode our quality of life. Worrying, holding on to hurts from the past, cognitive inflexibility, and rigidity may not send you to the therapist, but they can make your life unnecessarily gloomy.

Biological pattern

Existing research in the past few years has shown a biological pattern associated with OCD, Brain SPECT (Single Photon Emission Computerized Tomography) studies have shown increased blood flow in the cingulate system, along with increased activity in the basal ganglia (often the anxiety component of the problem).

SPECT is a sophisticated nuclear medicine study that looks directly at cerebral blood flow and indirectly at brain activity. SPECT studies show which parts of the brain are activated when we laugh, sing, cry, visualize or perform other functions. These studies help in diagnosis of cancer, head trauma, dementia, mood disorders, strokes seizures as well as several other conditions.

Like most forms of psychiatric illness, part of effective treatment for OCD often involves medication. At the time of writing this, there are eight 'antiobsessive medications' and more on the way. In addition to behaviour therapy the current medications that have shown effectiveness with OCD are Anafranil (clomipramine), Prozac (fluoxetine), Effexor (venalafaxine), Serzone (nefazodone), Remeron (mirtazapine) and Luvox (fluvoxamine). These medicines have provided many patients with profound relief from OCD symptoms.

Medications are often very helpful in the cingulate part of the brain, especially those medications that modulate the neurotransmitter serotonin. Medications that increase serotonin in the brain are termed serotonergic. These include Prozac, Zoloft, Paxil, Anafranil, Effexor, Remeron, Serzone, Desyrel and Luvox.

Several research studies have shown that when these medications are effective, they normalize activity in the cingulate system. Clinically, these medications decrease a patient's repetitive thoughts and compulsive behaviour, and relax people who have a tendency to be frozen by their inability to see options. When these medications work, they often have a dramatic effect on thoughts and behaviours.

Medications don't work all the time, and sometimes they have side effects that can be annoying and even disturbing. Yet, serotonergic medications are some of the new and most effective weapons in the arsenal against emotional pain and suffering. They have helped millions of people lead normal lives.

In addition, Saint-John's-Wort, a natural herbal treatment, can also be very helpful in raising Serotonin levels and calming the cingulate part of the brain. Saint-John's-Wort has been studied head to head with several antidepressants and found to be just as effective and with few side effects.

It has been used for many years in Germany, where it is prescribed seven times more often than Prozac. The usual dose of Saint-John's-

Wort is 300 mg (containing 0.3 per cent hypericin) three times a day. Saint-John's-Wort seems to be a very helpful treatment.

Low serotonin levels and increased cingulate activity are often associated with worrying, moodiness, emotional rigidity and irritability. There are two ways that food can increase serotonin levels. Foods high in carbohydrate, such as pastas, potatoes, bread, pastries, pretzels and popcorn, increase L-tryptophan levels (the natural amino acid building block for Serotonin) in the blood, resulting in more L-tryptophan being available to enter the brain, where it is converted to serotonin. The calming effect of serotonin can often be felt in thirty minutes or less by eating these foods.

Cerebral serotonin levels can also be raised by eating foods rich in tryptophan, such as chicken, turkey, salmon, beef, peanut, butter, eggs, green peas, potatoes and milk.

Many individuals unknowingly trigger cognitive inflexibility or mood problems by eating diets that are low in L-tryptophan. For example, the high-protein, low-carbohydrate diets that are recommended for low-dopamine states (related to prefrontal cortex under activity) often make cingulate problems worse. L-tryptophan is a relatively small amino acid. When you eat a high-protein diet, the larger amino acids compete more successfully to get into the brain, causing lower levels of brain serotonin and more negative emotional reactiveness (the role of L-tryptophan is still considered controversial and does not still have the therapeutic credibility of say St. John's Wort).

Nutritional supplements of L-tryptophan can also be very helpful. L-tryptophan was taken off the market a number of years ago because one contaminated batch, from one manufacturer, caused a rare muscle disease and a number of deaths. The L-tryptophan actually had nothing to do with the deaths. L-tryptophan is a naturally occurring amino acid found in milk, meat and eggs. Many patients have found it very helpful for improving sleeps, decreasing aggressiveness and improving mood control.

In addition, it does not have side effects, which gives it an advantage over antidepressants. L-tryptophan was recently reapproved by the United State's Food and Drug Administration. Doctors recommend L-tryptophan in doses of 1,000-3,000 mg to be taken at bedtime.

There have also been some recent studies with inositol, from the Vitamin B family. If given a dose of 12 to 20 mg a day, it has been shown to decrease moodiness, depression and problems of over-focus. To sum up, obsessive compulsive neuroses (particularly hypochondriasis) remain one of the biggest challenges of modern medicine. These patients remain in that twilight zone between diseases causing mortality and disorders that cause agony and mental hardship to themselves as well as to those dealing with them.

In terms of quality of life lost, the loss is incalculable for in the absence of such a malady, patients who are essentially normal people would have given off the best years of their lives to society and to themselves.

Saddled, however, as they are with this strange affliction, which the medical community does not take seriously, untold misery is being caused to millions of people. It is rather ironical that even men trained in medicine, who should be the first to recognize the suffering being experienced by these people, contemptuously brush it aside as an eccentric aspect of a patient's personality that need not be taken into account while treating him for physical ailments.

On the other hand, what a mature physician or surgeon should recognize and realize is that OCD is as painful to the victim, if not more, than a tumour or appendicitis or a pathological condition like infective hepatitis (to a person contracting that virus).

To laugh away the troubles of patients suffering from OCD or even to make them the butt of ridicule is not only uncalled for but shows an utter disregard for human dignity. The wise and experienced physician who encounters a patient suffering from OCD in addition to a physical ailment must in fact go out of the way to give him mental assurance and courage in the manner in which Hypocrites, the Father of Medicine, envisaged.

In a sense, the hypochondriac who imagines he has cancer of the stomach suffers more agony than a victim who is really afflicted with the disease; that being the case, physicians should perhaps gear their resources to reduce the mental agony of these patients rather than contemptuously drive them out from the consulting rooms and clinics all over the world.

27. *Plight of People in Twilight Zone*

> As a people we have become obsessed with health. There is something fundamentally, radically unhealthy about all this. We do not seem to be seeking more exuberance in living as much as staving off failure putting off dying. We have lost all confidence in the human body.
>
> LEWIS THOMAS

Man has never been successful in his war against disease as in the previous century. Almost all infections that used to wipe out vast sections of population were checked and a few eliminated. Only cancer and heart attack still elude conquest—thanks to our faulty life-style and some genetic factors. AIDS also has emerged, threatening the future of the race itself. No cure is yet in sight.

The stubbornness of a disturbing mental condition known as obsessive compulsive disorder (OCD), a form of neurosis, defying treatment, is rather ironical. Among the manifestations of OCD, 'hypochondriasis' is the most painful. OCD is the general term for two distinct inter-related disorders, obsessions and compulsive behaviour.

Obsessions are morbid thoughts a person cannot get rid of however hard he tries, like the fear that he has a particular disease or a terror of heights or closed spaces. Compulsive behaviour manifests itself in repeatedly touching objects, uttering words or checking taps. Of all these, hypochondriasis, the persistent preoccupation with the possibility of having one or more serious diseases, to the point of being incapable of concentrating on anything else, is the most agonizing. It may just appear as an eccentricity or a nuisance but in the sufferer's mind there is a hell. Two aspects make it intolerable: the patient's obsessive fear of having become afflicted with a terminal illness and a simultaneous lack of courage to go in for an investigation, for fear his suspicion may be confirmed. If the person suffers from any of the familiar ailments, such as a disorder of the stomach, or throat or urinary tract or exhaustion while climbing, there is a tendency on the part of the doctor to merely treat the physical ailment and prescribe a tranquillizer for the mental component which does nothing to solve the real problem.

In the post-Freudian era, hypochondriasis as well as other anxiety neuroses were explained away as 'punishments', subconsciously being inflicted by a person on himself for some guilt. Neuro-science has now disproved this and shown that the neurotransmitter called serotonin is the villain. Neurotransmitters carry messages from one neuron (nerve cell) to another by settling in the 'synapses', the gaps, between the cells. This makes 'adaptive' behaviour possible. If the nerve cells do not allow serotonin to remain there, but reabsorb them through receptors called 'reuptake pumps', the person concerned would lose his ability to see options. He would get stuck on thoughts like a broken record—the result, an 'obsession'.

Hypochondriasis, like other obsessions, remains one of the biggest challenges to medicine, mainly due to a lack of awareness of the functioning of the human brain and also partly because of the callous attitude of doctors (barring a few) who are reluctant to devote their time and energy to an ailment, the treatment of which may not be remunerative. However, some new drugs like Prozac which block the reuptake pumps and prevent reabsorption of serotonin, combined with behaviour therapy seem to offer hope.

But hypochondriasis is a chronic illness and so prolonged treatment may be necessary. Hypochondriacs remain in the twilight zone between terminal diseases and other illnesses which respond to treatment. What is worse, they are the butt of ridicule and jokes. Even doctors who should be the first to sympathize with them not only do not take them seriously but also chide them for their fears. Besides being inhuman, such an attitude also shows lack of respect for the dignity of human life.

In a hard-hitting article written in *Newsweek* three years ago, Chris Marrou, TV newscaster of Texas, drew attention to precisely this aspect and called for dropping the words like 'anxiety' and 'panic' while referring to society's attitude towards mental disorders, arguing that even death would be a sweet release compared to the agony of these patients, which according to him only another victim of mental illness can understand.

Condemning the stigma attached to mental sickness, he expressed a fond hope that a future presidential candidate's battle against depression or anxiety would be considered a mark of courage, instead of something to be hidden, and that Prozac could be swallowed openly without embarrassment by people who need it just as a patient with blood pressure takes a beta blocker today.

28. *Cellphones: Hazardous to Health?*

Just when the entire world had begun to rejoice that innovations in technology (as opposed to the usual pattern of rewarding success in basic research) like the cellphone had been recognized by the Nobel committee, we have received the rather unpalatable news that recent findings have revealed that there is an element of truth in the suspicion harboured by that many scientists that cellphones emit radiation waves that can harm human tissue.

Radio waves which are non-ionizing and are therefore different from X-rays (which damage cells by converting their atoms into ions . . . by depriving them of the electrons) are also quite dangerous at the high levels found in radar and inside microwave ovens. Now it seems cellphones also join that group.

The radiation from cellphones is measured in terms of watts per kilogram absorbed by a gram of human tissue. On this scale Ericsson T28 gives off the maximum at a level of 1.49 while Motorola Star Tac 7860 gives off the minimum at a level of 0.26—both being less than the safety threshold prescribed by the US federal communication commission.

There were more than 500 million cellphones in use in the world a few years ago. A rough estimate that another 200 million cellphones are being added every year, making this 50 billion dollar industry geared to produce the most popular product in history—a product which outsells computers, digital diaries, TVs and pagers put together. Despite the findings of an Australian researcher, based on his studies on mice, which developed tumours after being exposed to this type of radiation and other similar studies conducted by a man hired by cell companies themselves, linking the use of cellphones to a rare type of brain tumour, scientists are reluctant to come out with an unimpeachable verdict regarding the health hazard posed by cellphones.

In the meantime, opinion is gradually gaining ground that at least children with their developing brains may comparatively absorb more radiation than adults, leading parents to put a ban on children using cellphones.

Another guideline (issued in England) suggests that cellphone user must resort to a land line whenever there is a choice and exhorts children not to make non-essential calls in addition to using headsets to protect the brain. This guideline also recommends use of a hands free extension for minimizing health risk, a practice being resorted to in our country already by some people for 'showing off' as it is known without probably realizing that they are protecting themselves. There could also be the kind of warning carried now by cigarette packets that cellphones are hazardous to health.

Notwithstanding all these health risks of warnings there may be no reduction in the figures of sales of cellphones, given their utility, convenience and privacy. On the other hand, instead of cost, slimness, size or battery life, safety may acquire relatively higher rating when a cellphone is purchased. In any case, cellphone addicts, whether they are executives, doctors, politicians or even philandering husbands can never be expected to give up this product which has brought about as great a revolution in the quality of life as the aeroplane and car and the other marvels of modern technology.

29. *Of the Healthy, the Unhealthy and the Docs*

O who can hold a fire in his hand
By thinking on the frosty caucasus ?
Or cloy the hungry edge of appetite
By bare imagination of a feast?
Or Wallow naked in December snow
By thinking on fantastic summer's heat?

SHAKESPEARE in *King Richard II*

The banished Bolingbroke says these lines in despair, meaning that mere imagination cannot enable one to bear the pangs of separation or pain. How easy it is for a man who has never personally experienced misery, to render unsolicited advice to ignore misery, to a person actually experiencing agony.

There are millions of people who sail through life without having had a single serious disease, thanks to nature's gift of a strong constitution at birth itself, with all the organs in 'Mint Condition'; of course they might have had the usual bouts of minor infections which last for a few days requiring no treatment. They reach adulthood unscathed with no residual effects.

These healthy individuals become incapable of appreciating sickness, to the point of being utterly indifferent to, and even contemptuous of, people suffering from various kinds of ailments. These are the extremely lucky persons, who while gorging themselves with mouth-watering dishes at a restaurant or a feast, take a look at the empty plates of their unfortunate brethren without even feeling sorry for them. On the other hand, they cannot even conceal their annoyance when they notice a person hesitating to taste some dish kept on the table, as though the latter's presence is an affront to their host's hospitality.

No wonder for these healthy specimens of the human race who have never had a single stomach ailment, life is a bowl of cherries and not a single moment is wasted. Each day is packed with entertainment and sumptuous feasts (they have the habit of describing each and every dish whether it is Shahi Kurma, or Panneer, Butter Masala (spicy Indian dishes) or straberry daiquiri (a cocktail) with a vivid gusto and enthusiasm in great detail). They have no pity for those afflicted with agonizing and chronic stomach disorders like irritable bowel Syndrome or 'Crohn's disease' or condemned to a restricted diet all their lives by 'diabetes', no sympathy for victims of 'Grandmal' who live in constant fear of another attack all their lives, or little children afflicted with pneumonia whose lungs knock at their ribs 'against the use of nature'.

I know a man who used to make fun of guests who did not eat well at parties due to some chronic ailments. He would wonder why they had bothered to come to the party spoiling the atmosphere. This man realized what it was to be sick much later, when he himself came down with a serious ailment when his courage vanished like a gambler's lucky streak.

Let us now come to doctors. By virtue of their profession they may be familiar with the symptoms, diagnostic procedures and treatment of most of the diseases, though they themselves cannot be expected to have had personal experience of every disease apart from their own quota of a few minor ailments. For example, a doctor may know how to treat infective hepatitis, but he himself might have never had it. This is where the problem arises because, when a patient having this terrible ailment, complains about lack of appetite or nausea, the doctor, for no fault of his, cannot experience the same distress. There will always be a gap between his own perception of the patient's agony and the actual suffering experienced by the patient.

In fact, this is true of almost all the diseases. This gap can never be closed and the only course open for the doctor is to lend a sympathetic ear to the patient's woes. Since treatment relies to a large extent on reassurance, a doctor who loses patience or snaps at a patient, howsoever number of times he repeats his symptoms, might as well stop practising, instead of giving up the noble principles on which the edifice of medical treatment is established.

30. *Drug Firms' 'Weight Criteria' Puzzling*

> The desire to take medicine is one feature that distinguishes man, the animal, from his fellow creatures.
>
> WILLIAM OSLER

I have always been puzzled, and even somewhat amused by the 'weight criteria' applied by pharmaceutical companies in manufacturing drugs and also the manner in which physicians prescribe them. Surely the Lord above would never have intended that drugs should be prescribed, only in multiples of five (even as decimals).

Why does a physician ask his patient to take two tablets of Cifran 500 mg every day instead of say 473 or 483 mg for treating a serious respiratory infection? Why does he prescribe Flagyl 400 mg twice a day instead of 388 mg? Would those 12 mg make a difference or is it that 388 mg would be quite effective but the extra 12 mg would not cause any harm but would save the drug companies the trouble of measuring minute doses in milligrams. I cannot think of any drug in the entire spectrum of pharmacopoeia which is not either manufactured or prescribed in this fashion.

I am not convinced by the general explanation that drug companies do in fact make a scientific study under controlled conditions and have chosen the option of multiples of five as the optimum figure for dispensing drugs, keeping all aspects in view. To illustrate this, let us refer to drugs in two categories: Immodium (Lopamide Hydrochloride) is prescribed for controlling diarrhoea in Irritable Bowel Syndrome.

Irritable Bowel Syndrome: In India the drug is available as capsules but in America it is available as a tablet (or 'kaplet' as they term it). Patient are asked to take two kaplets first and then one kaplet after each movement of the bowel, assuming the diarrhoea is not viral or due to bacteria. But there are so many conditions such as 'irritable bowel syndrome', gastritis, colitis or conditions of extreme anxiety which can affect the Gastro Intestinal tract and trigger off a bout of diarrhoea. The trouble with immodium is that an overdose may give sudden relief only to result in a relapse. No drug manual mentions anything about a 'maintenance dose' in chronic diarrhoea, so that the frequency neither hampers normal activities, nor immobilizes the gut completely; the best course of action would be an 'adjustment' of dosage, i.e. by the patient himself by trial and error, something no doctor will advise him to do since immodium may not be manufactured in that particular desired strength. In fact almost all patients of irritable bowel syndrome resort to this method with or without the knowledge or consent of their physician and do benefit by their approach!

Erectile Dysfunction: Let us take a look at Viagra the miracle drug that cures erectile dysfunction. Erection in the human male is caused by erotic thoughts or acts stimulating nitric oxide which activates two enzymes causing smoothening of the penile muscles facilitating flow of blood into the erectile chambers. At the appropriate stage, another enzyme phosphate dieterase 5 gets activated to counter this effect, bringing down the erection, by causing 'backflow of blood'. When Viagra is taken the action of phosphate dieterase 5 is blocked, causing blood to remain in the penis resulting in a 'sustained erection'.

But here comes the problem. Doctors prescribe Viagra in three doses 25 mg, 50 mg or 100 mg warning the patient not to take it if he is using nitrates for a heart condition. It would cause a severe drop in Blood Pressure resulting even in death). So, one wonders why drug companies do not manufacture Viagra in various strength, i.e. 5 mg, 10 mg, 15 mg, 20 mg, 30 mg, 35 mg, etc., so that the dosage can gradually be increased to the point where the tablet is 'effective' for achieving penetration but will not let the BP fall so low as to be dangerous. I have questioned many urologists and doctors but I have not received a satisfactory explanation except that what I have suggested makes sense.

Additive: Another question about Viagra is that, as it lowers blood pressure, why all this fuss, about nitrates and weak hearts. Why not prescribe it as a 'drug of choice' for BP itself in the case of people who have Erectile Dysfunction also, killing two birds with one stone. Why give a person a betablocker or a calcium channel antagonist or any other drug for blood pressure and worry whether the 'additive' effect of Viagra may cause low blood pressure and death? Just do away with the other drugs and prescribe only Viagra!

31. *The Family Doctor*

> Doctor, no medicine—we are machines made to live—organized expressly for that purpose—such is our nature—Do not counteract the living principle—Leave it at liberty to defend itself, and it will do better than your drugs.
>
> NAPOLEON

Long before the so called 'multi-speciality' hospitals mushroomed everywhere in most of our major cities, and sophisticated diagnostic techniques like Magnetic Resonance Imaging and Computerized Axial Tomography scanning revolutionalized medical procedure, it was the family doctor or the general practitioner to whom everyone turned for medical treatment. He was a familiar figure in the pre-independence era and for at least two decades just after independence, driving an old motor vehicle, and stopping at each house to treat the sick, as well as to have a friendly chat with all the members of the family. He was a personal friend of the head of the family but he intimately knew all the members of the household by their names, ages and their mutual relationships.

In an era when the range of medicines in pharmacopoeia was not extensive and the practice of medical profession was largely empirical, the General Practitioner though conversant with all the known drugs of that period and was willing to apply them when really necessary, believed only in simple prescriptions and remedies allowing the body's immunity to fight infection. He carried a small wooden box, inside which were kept all the medical equipment, he needed a stethoscope (still regarded as the greatest diagnostic tool for a doctor) and a few emergency medicines. His clinical acumen was very sound and diagnosis unerring and he did not like to subject the patient to a battery of tests. He had a vast knowledge of medicine as a physician and excellent skill as a surgeon. A deep sense of humanity characterized his attitude towards treating the sick, and this was even more pronounced in respect of the poor from whom he would never accept money, literally practising what the great Charaka had preached 'Not for money or any earthly objects should one treat patients'.

Coming back to the family scene all the members of the family confided in him as he was the emotional bridge between them and paterfamilias. His opinion was sought on all matter's, e.g. education, career and marriage. He would be invited to all family functions and it was not uncommon for someone to receive aid for some ailment then and there itself.

His modest Nursing Home was like a Rishi's Ashram and he was always available day and night. A phone call was enough to make him come to a patient's residence promptly. He would treat the poor free of cost. Thus the poor as well as the rich had equal access to the full benefit of his therapeutic expertise. Such were these wonderful people who had dedicated their whole lives to the relief of human suffering. Handicapped by diagnostic tools of limited capability, they had to rely only on their observation and skill.

In his powerfully eloquent book 'How we die' distinguished American surgeon and physician Sherwin Nuland, observes that 'each one of us needs a guide who know us well as he knows the pathways by which we can approach death. There are so many ways to travel through the same thickets of disease so many choices to make, so many stations at which we may choose to take rest, continue or end the journey completely—until the last step of that journey we need the company of those we love and we need the wisdom to choose the way that is ours alone. This clinical objectivity that should enter into our decisions must come from a doctor familiar with our values and the lives we have led and not just from the virtual stranger whose super-specialized biomedical skills we have called upon.' Arguing that at such times it is not the kindness of strangers we need but the understanding of a long medical friend Sherwin Nuland makes a passionate plea for the resurrection of 'Family Doctors', a breed that has vanished forever from the medical horizon.

32. *Homeopathy: The Great Hoax*

Like Cures Like.

HANEMANN C.F.S.

If Astrology, by successfully encroaching into the hallowed field of astronomy, has been able to make millions of people all over the world take avoidable decisions with respect to love life, career and jobs, there is another pseudo-science which has had a similar degree of success in the medical field by exploiting the gullible and the ignorant, and even the educated and the intelligentsia who lack scientific temper. I am referring to homeopathy, the brain child of a German doctor, Samuel Christian Hahnemann, who in 1810 came out with a new theory of medical treatment and earned for himself the position of 'Emperor of Quacks'.

Before discussing Hahnemann's theory, it is necessary to explain why unlike professional astrologers, medical quacks find their task easy. There are two factors. First of all, most of the diseases that afflict us are self-limiting and disappear with practically no treatment. (A cold can be cured with medicines in seven days and without medicines in a week!) I am not taking into consideration those few cases where secondary complication arises and have to be controlled by medical intervention. In addition, a clever doctor can impress the gullible by sitting in a posh room with walls filled with awe-inspiring certificates, most of which are from institutions he himself had founded, dropping exotic Latin names like 'inferior vena cava', 'patella', 'Malleus', 'Larynx', 'Oesophagus', 'Caecum' so on and so forth, and recommending unnecessary tests and, to top it all, keeping a pretty girl as secretary to serve coffee or tea.

And second, many ailments are psychosomatic in origin. If a doctor, like the one referred to above, sincerely appears to listen to an elderly lady's woes and writes out a prescription containing a placebo (a harmless, inactive substance) he clinches the issue and wins her everlasting confidence. His fame spreads and soon her entire circle of friends becomes his ambassadors. One interesting aspect of human nature is that when most of your friends are claiming the expertise of a particular doctor, you would not like to be left out as a non-believer, just us you would like to claim seeing a particular star even when you haven't, simply because others are claiming to have seen it. Thus the cult of homeopathy has grown from strength to strength and spread its tentacles far and wide.

The first great principle of homeopathy is the 'law of similia', according to which a drug will cure a disease if the same drug given to a healthy person will produce symptoms similar to the disease. This implies giving a drug in increasing concentrations until symptoms appear and if these symptoms are similar to those of known ailments the drug is considered effective in curing those ailments. Again for some unknown reason, each individual is considered unique irrespective of the disease and is treated according to the symptoms.

Secondly, homeopathic medicines are given in inconceivably minute doses. The smaller the dose the more potent it is supposed to be. Compounds are diluted to one decillionth, i.e. a millionth of a million. This is like letting a drop of the medicine to fall into the Atlantic Ocean, mixing it and taking out a spoonful.

Hahnemann believed that as the drug becomes less material it vanishes and acquires 'spiritual' powers. He even recommended diluting it till not a single molecule of the original substance remained. The controversy over dosage split homeopaths into two groups—the 'purists' who followed Hahnemann and the 'low potency' men who thought it necessary to preserve at least a few molecules. Again purists of today have replaced the spiritual powers theory with another concept of 'radiations' which remain after a substance vanishes. This does not seem to be entirely without a physical basis for reasons not yet fully understood.

If homeopaths like to claim that their law of similia has an analogy in vaccination: their infinitesimal theory also has some factual basis in respect of a small number of drugs. What homeopaths have done is to exaggerate both these limited truths to the point of absurdity. Many homeopathic drugs are made out of skunk secretions, crushed live bed bugs, powdered starfish, uric acid obtained from human urine, and snake excrements. Scientific analysis by pharmacologists has shown that in the extremely diluted quantities in which these drugs are taken, they cause neither harm nor cure. But that is not the point. A medicine is given only for the purpose of curing a disease and not because it does not do any harm.

Homeopaths also cite cases where someone who has been on allopathic drugs either dies or fails to recover. This may be due to the fact that the patient was too weak, or because he had started the course too late or because even allopathy cannot have a 100 per cent success rate. This is where the homeopath will step in and say that had the patient been given homeopathic drugs he would have been cured.

Another favourite theme of homeopaths is that all antibiotics are poisons and should be avoided. One wonders how many millions of soldiers would have died if Penicillin had not been administered.

Homeopaths today make full use of allopathy in diagnosis and surgery. Ironically, they have diluted the amount of homeopathy in the curriculum until homeopathic educational institutions have evolved into potent full-fledged modern medical schools, a rather hypocritical situation to be in, for a pseudo-science that began its history by criticizing allopathy and advocating 'diluting' as its main principle.

33. *A Life Charged with Intellect Courage and Truth: A Tribute to S. Jay Gould*

Several months ago, one small news item appeared in most of the newspapers in the country and some reputed foreign magazines. Given the length of the column and the manner in which it was written it might not have attracted much attention. Many people might have missed it and even those who read it might not have attached much significance to the contents.

This was really pathetic, considering that the column had mentioned in a routine fashion the death of Stephan Jay Gould, arguably the greatest evolutionary bio-scientist of the previous century—which should have certainly deserved a better treatment.

Some years ago, when Gould had gone for a medical check-up for some ailment, some tests had been performed. Gould had noticed a certain reluctance on the part of the medical investigation team, particularly one nurse, to give him the implications of the result of the investigation. He was merely told what in the opinion of the medical staff a patient ought to know (apparently, they did not know his stature as a great medical scientist).

However, having overheard a medical term, he went to the library of the Harward University. On perusing the relevant medical books, Gould found out the reason why he had not been told the truth by the investigating group. He had been afflicted with a rare form of abdominal cancer which, even among malignant tumours, had the reputation for the swiftness with which it claimed the life of its victim.

But without panicking, he calmly went about reading all the facts related to that cancer. With scientific precision, he worked out the life-span available to him using statistical probability. Gould found out that he had a chance to live for many more years if luck held. This is precisely what happened. After a long fight with cancer, he died only recently.

But then Gould was an extraordinary man of rare moral courage. In his many books he was outspoken and hard-hitting, condemning intellectual dishonesty and deliberate actions taken on the basis of misinterpretation of scientific findings, such as a man called Goddard had done with the results of Intelligence Quotient tests in early part of the last century, to restrict immigration of Jew into America.

(IQ tests had been devised to select people who needed extra help—not to identify morons, so it had no other scope.) The mind boggles at the thought of how many Einstein had been refused entry into America because of Goddard and his team! Gould's book, 'The Mismeasure of Man', clearly brings out this point.

Gould was born in New York city in 1941 to a Hungarian court stenographer. The sight of the Tyrannosaurus Rex at the American Museum of Natural History aroused his interest in biology when he was a five-year-old boy. Completing his Ph.D at Columbia in 1967, he moved to Harward where he became professor of Geology and curator of the Harward Museum of comparative zoology.

In 1973, Gould used the fossils of the Burgess shale to theorise that evolution is not a ladder of predictable progress but a copiously branching bush continually pruned by the grim reaper of extinction! Working, in the West Indies for many years, he put forth the theory of 'Punctuated Equilibrium' which views evolution as 'episodic' rather than 'continuous'.

Nevertheless, he was a supporter of Darwin and was against 'Creationism', which he discouraged from being taught in schools, a stand vindicated by the judiciary. Gould's many books popularized science, and brought complex theories requiring rigorous scientific discipline within the reach of the common reader.

Till the very last moment, Stephen Jay Gould had the courage of conviction to take an uncompromising stand on truth, which after all, is the quintessential aspect of science.

His battle with cancer is just one example of his heroic attitude in which the dignity of one brave man triumphed over death—even if it claims all our lives in the end.

PART III

OUR COUSINS IN AMERICA

34. *Style of Life of Indians Settled in America: NRI Syndrome of Unsolicited Comments*

In the late 1950s and early 1960s, Indian society witnessed a rather interesting phenomenon—the tendency to regard any person returning to the country from abroad after a visit, or any person of Indian origin living abroad visiting our country, as some kind of a privileged human being. This was because of the enormous number of restrictions imposed to conserve foreign exchange, including the rules to regulate travel of Indians to foreign countries resulting in a shortage of foreign consumer goods shortly after India obtained independence, which naturally elevated the status of those who could go abroad and bring back those commodities.

This was particularly noticeable in colleges where, for example, a boy wearing a 'nylon shirt' as it was called or possessed a Wilson tennis racket was the centre of attraction.

Those who did not go abroad had to be content with ordinary shirts and rackets.

Apart from this, the 'foreign returned' boy seemed to have a superior air about him which defined the exclusivity of a special breed which had access to foreign goods. They would speak about exciting experiences in other countries, shiny cars, exotic brands of whisky, chocolates and cheese, and films and programmes on the television, which had not yet come to India.

Some of those students who had gone to America for higher studies chose to stay back, making for themselves lucrative careers. While enjoying fully the American way of life, they still looked towards India for music, sarees, pickles and often brides. This trend continued till the 1980s, getting the best out of both the countries—praising every aspect of America and simultaneously criticizing the disorganization, disease and dirt which according to them were the only features of this country which had embraced a faulty political ideology and disastrous economic policy after independence, leading the country to chaos and making it uninhabitable. (It was not a question of what was wrong with India. It was a question, of what was right.) In their eyes their own country had become, over the years, a land of poverty, hunger, disease, filth, crowded trains, and buses which ran late, ramshackle cars, defective telephones, substandard medical facilities and erratic electricity supply. What excuse could six hundred million people have in not achieving excellence in a single field. It was beyond their comprehension how anyone could live in such a country whose problems could never be solved. Nor could they shake off India from their thoughts. They were obsessed with the political and economic developments in India, commenting on how such and such politician could have handled a particular crisis in a better manner. They gave out their views on the Indian political scenario with an air of finality which no Indian professor or journalist could.

But among these arrogant people there were many who would make an annual visit to India to see their parents and relations even if they felt that there was the danger of their contracting malaria or dysentery. These included some who would make an occasional flattering reference to something Indian, like a garment which even though available in America did not quite match the texture and quality of the same garment being sold in a certain obscure shop, say in Chennai. After all, they were honest enough in giving the devil its due. America had skyscrapers, freeways, rollercoasters, the biggest theme park and departmental stores, but when it came to the garment in question ('a mull veshti' a long piece of cotton cloth worn round the waist and legs by men), 'that' store in Chennai had a definite edge. Hence, even if they bought suits, shirts, ties, shoes, watches and cameras in America, their 'mull veshti' had to be purchased from that particular shop in India, a gesture that reflected their intellectual honesty, humility and patriotism.

35. *Style of Life of Indians Settled in America: Brains to Bronze*

Among the hordes, who had gone to America four or five decades ago for higher education or professional career or pure research and settled there, many have become affluent doctors or prominent lawyers or eminent professors in some of the great universities. Having sucked the marrow out of American life for decades, it is these people who have taken upon themselves the task of preaching about the values of India's culture and art not to Americans but ironically to the ordinary Indian student from a middle-class household who has a genuine need and a justifiable desire to go to America for higher studies to improve his prospects.

According to these people, our students should remain in India, the land that gave the world the concept of zero, the number system, the most accurate value of pi (π) and the decimal and place systems, long before Europe had even woken up to become one civilized entity. One arrogant and cheeky Indian Professor in America, who considers himself an authority on ancient Indian Art asked me, why Indians were coming to New York to gaze at the skyscrapers and the Statue of Liberty instead of admiring the Taj Mahal, the 'dew drop on the cheek of time'? Why were they praising Mount Rushmore instead of feeling proud about Mahabalipuram? Why were they going into ruptures over the Venus de Milo instead of recognizing the beauty of Chola bronzes? They were a misguided lot who had to be educated about the culture of India. And therefore our 'cultural ambassadors' who themselves had attained enlightenment, only after swimming in milk and honey for three or four decades in America, were the best qualified to preach to our young, naive and ignorant students about India's cultural heritage. If they did not expose how Western historians had deliberately distorted facts to credit every major scientific discovery, including the computer, to their own scientists, instead of ancient India and the blatant plagiarism indulged in by Emerson or reveal the intricacies of Vedic mathematics, posterity would never forgive them! Indeed it was not merely the students but even grown up people from all walks of life who had to be educated about India's glorious past.

However it was another matter that not one of these enlightened Indians of America has even a rudimentary knowledge of the literature of any of India's major languages, or a genuine insight into Hindu mythology, or Hindu civilization. All that they have is a meagre 'awareness' of our country's culture and art obtained by glancing through glossy brochures or books, tailor-made for foreigners and which are usually found in the bookshops of five star hotels!

And this 'awareness' which has dawned on them in the light of their own nostalgia and a sense of guilt at having deserted their motherland and spoken ill about it for several years, has driven them to this stage of 'reverse patriotism'.

In any case, we do not need their sermons on India's culture now. We have in our own country intellectual giants steeped in the Vedas and the Upanishads, people whose feats of memory in reciting poetry in Sanskrit or Telugu or any other language is unirivalled, in this planet and whose knowledge of Indian art does not depend on the interpretation of some professor in Connecticut or California.

It is in this context that one must view the profound theories of some of our brethren in the New World. No doubt they are outstanding and eminent in their respective fields but what makes their theories questionable are their motives and attitudes a certain patronizing air of superiority that seems to tell all of us here that 'they' know about it whereas 'we' don't.

There is another aspect to this. Having reached the heights in their chosen profession, some of these scientists and engineers have begun to explain the scientific aspect of art, if not the artistic aspect of science! They interpret the flashes of thought in the Indian sculptor's brain that had conceived the eroticism in Parvati's coy posture and the harmony in Shiva's Cosmic Dance captured in a Chola bronze as reflections of the brain's infinite ability to perceive the aesthetic values or synaesthetic significance of certain curves and lines that define Parvati's perfect breasts and hips and Shiva's masculine limbs, not to mention the deliberate intention of the sculptor to exaggerate the size and shape of some organs and reduce the same of some others to achieve certain effects.

These are the same people who while visiting a state, say Rajasthan today, stay in the Rambagh Palace Hotel or the Lake View Palace Hotel and rave about the luxuries not to be found any where else in the world and gush about the hospitality lavished on them by erstwhile Maharajahs and clever hoteliers who produce for them the playful baby elephants, the docile cobras and the sadhus clad in tiger skin while nubile Silken girls wearing diaphanous costumes serve sherbet, tandoori chicken, biryani and even champagne. After all, the dream created by their own dollars shields from them the dead livestock and camels in the villages, the tired women walking for miles for a bucket of water, and the fact that the state has been reeling under a drought for years. Unfortunately, what is displayed to them and what actually is the state of affairs are two sides of the same coin!

See them again at a glance our fellow countrymen, caught between two worlds, not sure whether they belong to America or India, making the typical gestures one frequently sees in American soap operas like shaking their heads or shrugging the shoulders or moving the hands in a particular manner, uttering superlatives like 'great' or 'fantastic' at the slightest provocation, speaking with a nasal twang, a limited vocabulary mostly containing unmentionable four letter words (when Rex Harrison said in 'My Fair Lady' that in America they have not spoken English for years, he was probably referring to this group!) If they are genuinely interested in helping their motherland, they are quite welcome and there are so many ways to do so. Otherwise someone ought to tell them they are not welcome here. They can continue to sit in the jacuzzis in their luxurious bathrooms, overlooking the Pacific Ocean watching whales migrate or mate, or continue to listen to Semmangudi or Bhimsen Joshi in their sports cars, while cruising down the Pacific coast highway, even while we all sit here and wonder where we had gone wrong in creating and exporting such an arrogant, patronizing, and confused breed as the Indian American!

36. *Style of Life of Indians Settled in America: More American than Americans*

While analysing the ethos of Indians settled in America, from the first person who had gazed with admiration at the skyscrapers in the early 1950s to the professors and executives of the 1990s who have taken upon themselves the task of preaching India's cultural heritage to Americas one cannot help noticing some peculiar traits of our brethren which are not only amusing but also at times annoying.

For instance, our countrymen there insist on fastening our seat-belts, failing which they even refuse to start the car. Now, no one doubts that seat-belts protect us in the event of an accident. But why do our cousins, who are so meticulous about following that rule in America, flout every rule under the Motor Vehicles Act while on a visit to India, and expect a friend who happens to be a senior police officer to use his influence to let them off ?

Why is it that in America they act as if they were ashamed of your conduct, should you carelessly drop a piece of paper somewhere in the house or on the road, and point out to you patronizingly the nearest trash can, whereas here they litter the guestroom with discarded gift-wraps.

Why is the decibel level of their voice kept below the threshold of human audibility in America, but raised to the loudness of a 'Tarzan jungle cry' in India? Why is it that even if absent mindedly you jump the queue in America they chide you saying 'you ought not to have done so', while in India they get all their work done with the help of influential friends or relations, let alone join a queue. And how is it that in America they are so punctual in attending any function or keeping appointments, whereas here they plead 'too many engagements in too short a time' as an excuse for systematically coming late to give audience to 'adoring' crowds! And why, again, do they use expressions like (a) 'Excuse me', (b) 'Is that right?' and (c) 'Sorry, come again?' with exaggerated courtesy while in the America, but think it more appropriate, while in India to switch to the more frequently used four-letter words in their limited vocabulary (of course they do sprinkle their boring narratives with an occasional 'the bottom line is . . .' or 'boy! What a success story . . .' with the aim of impressing their old schoolmates.

They also have a tendency to use high jargon while referring to normal everyday things—children at home having 'sibling rivalry' or experiencing 'peer pressure' at school.

And take their rather annoying obsession with a sport that is a pathetic imitation of cricket—just imagine Bradman's game played without stumps and bails and overs and teams named after native Indian Tribes, e.g. 'Apache Braves', 'Cherokee sluggers'.

We do appreciate their enthusiastic observance of Father's Day and Mother's Day but how, when and why did they give up Deepawali! They are more American than Americans themselves when in New Jersey or Detroit, and less Indian than even Americans when in Chennai or Bangalore!

Next time anyone quotes Scott:

> Breathes there the man, with soul so dead,
> Who never to himself hath said,
> This is my own, my native land!
> Whose heart hath ne'er within him burn'd
> As home his footsteps he had turn'd
> From wandering on a foreign strand!

We should unhesitatingly point our fingers at our cousins in America.

37. *Style of Life of Indians Settled in America: Our Affluent Cousins*

One conspicuous aspect anyone can notice is that despite being one of the largest and most affluent communities in America, our cousins, i.e. Indian settled in America have not formed a 'strong lobby with clout' in the sense the Jews, the English, the Italians and some others have done.

True, they meet at temples or for bhajans and do visit each other, in fact to the point of excluding others and exposing themselves to the charge of being clannish. At these gatherings, the conversations revolve around an analysis of the performance of the Indian government or Indo-American relations. But nothing concrete emerges, and they realize that their weekend is coming to a close and a new week of toil, tears and sweat is about to begin.

Before we come to the 'weekend syndrome' let us have a look at what we mean by a 'lobby with clout'. New York, for instance, is the financial capital of the world. It is generally acknowledged that the Jews in New York, with their enormous wealth and power, can even influence decisions taken in the White House.

Similarly, the English, by virtue of their common ties with America, receive royal treatment in every field of interaction, whereas our cousins have to endure the slings and arrows of bureaucratic or other types of hassles at every stage. But being essentially law abiding and also affluent they manage to stay away from trouble, unlike for instance the Hispanic groups. They basically operate as small families, each consisting of four or five good citizens whose mental horizon does not extend beyond the boundaries of the lawns of their houses.

However, this very limitation imposes a restriction on their capacity to have a major say in anything, not even the kind of meal that is to be served by any major airline. The next time you are on a flight across the Atlantic and notice the foreigner sitting next to you enjoying the food he had ordered, including his favourite juicy steak, whereas you have to accept whatever the stewardess thrusts on your table—uncooked lentils and corn smelling of rancid butter and unrecognizable vegetables floating in stale yogurt with a label 'special meal' stuck to the foil, adding insult to injury please try to understand that our meek cousins in New York and Los Angeles have never had the courage to tell any airline that what they are serving can by no stretch of imagination be called a special vegetarian meal, for it does not even have one item from the thousands of mouth-watering dishes that constitute Indian vegetarian food; nor even that we are not monkeys to be fed with bananas and peanuts throughout the flight.

Let us now take the 'Mall obsession'. A mall is a collection of various kinds of shops located in a building of enormous area and size. The first time you visit a mall you get the feeling that you are in heaven. Your host will take you to the mall on the way to his workplace and pick you up when he returns home. But after few visits, the novelty wears off and you would even like to avoid the mall! You keep hearing from your cousins the rather childish claim that 'our mall is the biggest in America' in every city you visit. All malls are alike and lack that personality and unique charm of some of the famous shops in London or Paris or America itself or the quaintness of little kiosks in Europe.

And now let us take the 'weekend syndrome'. From Monday morning it is one mad rush for our cousins—traffic jams, meetings and conferences; with hardly a minute to relax in their tiny cubicles and plan out the programme for the coming weekend. And once the weekend arrives, Saturday is reserved for household chores, polishing their cars, attending to plumbing jobs and other minor repairs. Only on a Sunday can our affluent cousins afford to have a proud glance at all their latest gadgets and call friends and relations in their motherland to discuss their next visit to India!

38. *Style of Life of Indians Settled in America: Hollywood and Our Cousins*

Like millions of Indian children, I had been seeing movies since boyhood. My earliest memories are of Charlie Chaplin imitating Hitler, Tarzan fighting a crocodile, and Sindbad blinding the Cyclops, which we all still enjoy. *Scaramouche* and *Robin Hood* came later—the violence confined to the lengthy sword-fight between Stewart Granger and Mel Ferrer in the former, and the sexual content to Errol Flynn passionately kissing Olivia De Havilland in the latter. The chariot race in *Ben Hur* and the destruction of the Philistine temple in *Samson and Delilah,* are unforgettable scenes in movie history.

After a few years we were considered mature enough to watch *Gone with the Wind.* We could hear our elders in the back rows discussing in hushed whispers, the seduction of Vivien Leigh by Clark Gable.

However, this is not the theme of this article as will become obvious. America is a nation of immigrants—a melting pot of races. The 'Pilgrim fathers' as well as the earliest immigrants had a historical and moral advantage over those who came later. The process of immigration continued in the following centuries. Jews from Russia, and later from Europe, and others constituted the majority in the first five decades of the last century. In the sixties, Indians started to go to America for higher education or employment. Their numbers gradually increased reaching the present stage—a large and affluent group, though not comparable population wise to the earlier hordes from Europe.

The bottom line (or 'bodom line' as our cousins pronounce it), is that they have done well for themselves and also served America well. The engineers, doctors, scientists, and businessmen, owning restaurants or shops selling a range of goods from jewellery, to electronic gadgets, provisions to sarees, are successful and affluent.

Then how and why is it that they have been completely ignored by Hollywood? Indians with American passports are no different from their American neighbours in Connecticut or California, who had migrated from Europe in the fifties. But in the thousands of films churned out by the world's greatest movie-producing empire, there is not a single film or television serial about an Indian family—no love-story, no thriller no comedy—nothing! Indians work in multinational corporations, educational institutions, hospitals, etc. Though clannish (in fact to the point of being rooted to their own family), they do interact with American society. In fact, there are a few interracial marriages, creating their own complications. So there is really no dearth of themes, considering the above scenario—issues relating to customs, habits and problems created by their mind, body and money ('*man*', '*tan*' and '*dhan*'—in Hindi) being in different countries. And even though their American passports are recognized by the Immigration, they do not exist as far as Hollywood is concerned! But our cousins do not seem to be unhappy either! They are quite contented, watching Michael Douglas making love to Sharon Stone and Hrithik Roshan courting Amisha Patel. The two pairs are in two separate compartments, one for 'genuine' Americans and another for 'synthetic' ones. See them again, our cousins rushing to a video rental store in 'Little India' in every city asking the owner 'Do you have *Kaho Na Pyar Hai* or *Lagaan*'? (as blockbuster outlets do not carry Indian movies). As long as such an attitude prevails, why should Hollywood bother to make a film about people from a nation it does not understand? For Hollywood knows that our cousins possess American passports only for staying in America and enjoying McWorld consumer benefits, but that their looks are 'Eastward turned' (to twist Milton's phrase a little)!

39. *Style of Life of Indians Settled in America: Adding Insulat to Injury*

My views on the style of life and behaviour pattern of our cousins settled in America as reflected in my articles had evoked a favourable response from people in India while not exactly pleasing our cousins. Some of the reactions of our cousins are given below:

A. I have made too sweeping a generalization which does not reflect the true state of affairs.

B. I live in a country with millions of people below the poverty line. We are in two separate compartments and I cannot understand the American ethos.

C. Visiting America often, is not the same as living there, and so I have no insight into the psychology of Americans.

D. As far as Hollywood is concerned why should it take films about a nation in which it is interested. After all Americans would like of various reasons to see movies relevant only to them, e.g. 'God-father' as it portrays the story of the Italian mafia, which is of interest to the average American, 'Three Coins in the Fountain' about three Americans in Rome (of course, our cousins have no explanation for 'Roman Holiday' or 'Don Juan' or 'Scaramouche'. If something sensational had occurred, e.g. 'Gandhi's Freedom Struggle', a film had in fact been made (which by the way was made by Richard Attenborough of England). They (Americans) are just not interested in people who have gone to America to enjoy a 'better life'. Schindler's List is important as it concerns Jews who are a major force to reckon with in America, but how is the Partition of India or the 'Emergency' in India of any interest to the average American? The life of a German composer (Amadeus) and the intrigue inside a Russian or British Royal Family is relevant but how on earth is the story of Ashoka (described by H.G. Wells as the greatest of Kings) of any interest to Hollywood?

Coming to food served on board Aeroplanes, I was very happy to hear that for Udadi (the Telugu New Year's day), the India Airlines managed to serve various delicacies enjoyed by Andhras such as 'pesarattu', 'Upma', etc. Then why should there be any difficulty for international carriers to follow the example of Indian Airlines? Why do they always serve the same combination of food items (undercooked rice on which is poured an yellowish concoction which can be interpreted as a 'Kurma' or a lentil soup and the same pieces of papaya, pineapple, and raw carrots—supposed to be a salad). Not only that—the same inedible fare is served for lunch, dinner and breakfast in all the sectors. The meals are given different names, e.g. Jain Meal, Asian Vegetarian Meal, Vegetarian Meal, etc., but you get the same stuff with marginal variations with no hope of the carrier giving you a 'samosa' or a cutlet or a 'dosa', let alone normal rice and 'Dal Makhani' while the Italian gets his pasta and the Chinese his noodles plus whatever he can get in Hong Kong.

I have deliberately chosen these two issues because they are the direct result of the utter inaction of out timid cousins. By arguing that for 'them' (Americans) we are inconsequential, our cousins are admitting the very charge that they think that they are refuting—inasmuch as they themselves are Americans. And this is exactly where they are missing the whole point. Instead of rushing to 'Little India' to get Lagaan or criticizing India day in and day out, why do they not spare a few hours to sell a good story or theme to Steven Spielburg.

Regarding the meal, their attitude seems to be why bother to convince a major Airline about the necessity to serve authentic Indian food when it is much easier to compromise on a trivial issue and eat whatever is thrown on their plate at an altitude of 40,000 feet. After all for our cousins the path of least approach is the best approach.

40. *Style of Life of Indian in America: Our Friendly Cousins*

> Americans are a very modern people, of course. They are a very open people too. They wear their hearts on their sleeves. They don't stand on ceremony. They take people as they are. They make no distinction about a man's background, his parentage, his education. They say what they mean and there is a vivid muscularity about the way they say it. They admire everything about them without reserve or pretence of scholarship. They are always the first to put their hands in their pockets. They press you to visit them in their own home the moment they meet you, and are irrepressibly good-humoured, ambitious and brimming with self-confidence in any company. Apart from all that I've got nothing against them.
>
> TOM STOPPARD in *New-Found-Land*

After having observed the habits and behaviour of our cousins in America for the last two decades cannot resist the temptation to spell out all their characteristic traits, in a similar fashion.

First and foremost a contempt for India which according to them is a land of disease, dirt, disorganization, corruption, poverty, defective telephones, erratic power supply, lack of medical facilities, cars and buses which are not road worthy, and trains and aeroplanes which run late, thanks to its faulty political system and disastrous economic policy. It is a society whose hallmarks are hypocrisy, an unhealthy curiosity, scandal and gossip, rudeness, intrusion into other people's privacy, lack of manners, delays and unwarranted interruptions in conversation.

On the other hand, America, the richest and most technologically advanced nation on earth, is a paradise of perfection, punctuality, excellence and cleanliness. All the same, our cousins continue to make their periodic visits to India to see their relative and friends and more importantly to 'collect' brides, pickles, Indian music cassettes and 'sarees', even while they 'pontificate' generously on the Indian political scene, e.g. how Gujarat has to be handled or on the way Indian should deal with Sri Lanka or the Middle East. (As fast as the American political system is concerned, our cousins do not exist and the highest political authority with whom they can claim to have an acquaintanceship is a senator!)

Let us now take up 'gestures', some of which I had mentioned briefly in earlier articles : the nodding or shaking of the head, the vertical or horizontal movement of the neck, the shrugging of the shoulders and the stretching of the arms wide apart during casual conversation, reflect a body language which may not look good even on Sean Connery and in the case of our cousins, is suggestive of a limited vocabulary developed around the objectionable four letter word, and then shit, crap, phoney, awesome, boy followed closely by phrases such as a 'good deal', 'it's great', 'is that right?' and 'I will get it' when the phone rings and that rare gem 'it's not just big, it's a big big !' (Shakespeare would turn in his grave) and the bottom line is, etc., and euphemistically sounding phrases to describe normal human emotions/actions, e.g. 'sibling rivalry', 'peer pressure', 'laidback', 'attitude', etc.

Every family regards itself as a 'Success Story' which is another favourite expression, Dad is a top executive in one of the greatest multinationals. Mom is a real estate dealer and they both earn millions of dollars. One son has recently joined Harward and another has received a certificate of merit from Yale or Columbia (who has the time or energy to verify these claims). They both represent their colleges in basketball and their heroes are Michael Jordan and Babe Ruth. Their houses cost 10 million dollars and they have four cars, a Mercedez, a Porche, a Lexus and a Mazda. The younger son lives on a steady diet of comics of Teenage Ninja Mutani Turtle. At least African Americans get a chance to appear as attorneys or judges in films, wherever our cousins are totally ignored by Hollywood as well as the television. But our cousins are not particularly bothered. Being timid they do not want to tell the authorities concerned about the type of food served as Asian meal by International Carriers but rationalize it saying, 'why bother to take up such trivial issue', and give up their hard-earned reputation as good citizens. And if you are also quite willing to overlook their 'weekend syndrome', 'mall fever', 'yard-sale obsession', 'good-deal fixation' and 'we can buy, attitude' you really should have nothing against our timid and insecure but affluent and friendly cousins in America.

By and large however, our cousins are a friendly people who are hospitable, law-abiding, hard working, and eagerly await the weekend, when they can attend to chores at home and call family and friends in India and go for a picnic or meet other families from India at 'bhajans' or in temples. The ambitious few become office-bearers of Tana, Rana, Kana or Bana (acronyms for Telugu Association of North America, etc.) which bring them in contact with visiting dignitaries from India.

PART IV

SHAKESPEARE AND LITERATURE

41. *The Scientist in Shakespeare*

> I believe the souls of five hundred Sir Isaac Newtons would go to the making up of a Shakespeare.
>
> SAMUAL TAYLOR COLRIDGE

I cannot claim to be a Shakespeare scholar. But since childhood, I have been his humble devotee, and not a single day passes without my reading a few quotations from his works and even if I do not read them, Shakespeare has become an addiction, with the result, I find compulsively reciting to myself a few lines that have become part of the treasures of the literary heritage of man. They have become so ingrained in my subconscious that they find their way into my writings because of their intrinsic excellence and not due to my special skills.

Science is a noble enterprise concerned with the 'how' of things which makes discovering the laws of nature its primary goal. Poetry, on the other hand, is a creative enterprise concerned with human emotions which makes a contemplation of the phenomena that affect them its main objective. Each has its own role in the scheme of things and no purpose is served by one encroaching upon the other. And indeed this has been the state of affairs for centuries.

But of late, thanks to the increased sophistication and specialization of certain branches of science one is beginning to notice a tendency on the part of some scientists to undertake patronizingly speculative exercises regarding the nature of art and even the evolution of the language of Shakespeare. On the other hand, there is evidence to show that centuries ago, by flashes of intuitive genius, Shakespeare had, in many of his plays, amazingly pre-empted some scientific truths. Limitations of space would allow me to cite only a few examples.

Cassius telling Brutus

> The fault, dear Brutus, is not in our stars
> But in ourselves, that we are underlings

at a time when Kepler, famous for his laws of planetary motion, himself believed in astrology, is amazing. Harvey discovered the circulation of blood but Brutus says to Portia in Julius Caesar:

> You are my true and honourable wife
> As dear to me as are the ruddy drops
> The visit my sad heart.

Julius Caesar observes elsewhere

> It seems to me most strange that men should fear:
> Seeing that death, a necessary end,
> Will come when it will come.

(The emphasis is on 'necessary end').

Modern biology supports this view that death is essential for the survival of the species and not just the inevitable end of life.

Duncan's lines in Macbeth

> There's no art
> To find the mind's construction in the face;
> He was a gentleman on whom I built
> An absolute trust.

is in tune with modern psychology.

A man who is unaware about his impending death finds nature beautiful. So Duncan says:

> This Castle hath a pleasant seat; the air
> Nimbly and sweetly recommends itself
> To our senses.

Macbeth is full of passages reflecting the nightmares, hallucinations and fears in a murderer's mind.

He asks the doctor:

> Canst then not minister to a mind diseased,
> Pluck from the memory a rooted sorrow,
> Raze out the written troubles of the brain
> And with some sweet oblivious antidote
> Cleanse the bosom of the perilous stuff,
> Which weighs upon the heart?

The doctor replies:

> Theirin the patient must minister to himself.

What a knowledge of psychology!

There are other examples also, such as the moon influencing the tides

The moist star
Upon whose influence Nepture's Empire stands

in Hamlet or

By medicine life may be prolong'd, yet death
Will seize the doctor too.

in Cymbeline, and the inferiority complex of Richard III which leads him to wickedness as compensation.

I, that am curtail'd of this fair proportion
Cheated of feature by dissembling nature,
Deform'd, unfinish'd, sent before my time
Into this breathing world, scarce half made up,
And that so lamely and unfashionable
That dogs bark at me as I halt by them.

I leave it to reader to decide as to who should analyse whose brain.

42. *Neuroscientists, Leave Shakespeare Alone!*

Nobel Laureate Peter Medawar has observed in his book 'The Limits of Science' that 'in terms of the fulfilment of declared intentions science is incomparably the most successful enterprise man has engaged upon', e.g. landing on the moon, curing certain diseases, designing computers. He opines that science's greatest glory is its unlimited power to answer questions of the kind it can answer. The emphasis is on 'declared intentions' and 'the kind of questions science can answer'. Science cannot answer riddles of existence or about man's task in the Universe, just as a car cannot fly, i.e. not perform a task for which it is not designed. Because of this limitation, it is to literature of philosophy that we must turn for answers.

About five decades ago it had been fashionable to interpret human behaviour in terms of psychology, thanks to Sigmund Freud and others. Writers like C.E.M. Joad had pointed out that the only mind to which a psychologist had access was his own. By introspection it was thought he could acquaint himself with its contents. But the mind he introspected was the same as the mind by means of which introspection was being performed, and so it was affected by the fact that it was being made the subject of inquiry. Neurophysiology should be having similar limitations though because of its knowledge of the brain's anatomy and success in curing certain ailments, it is in a relatively superior position.

Let us now look at synkinesia (mimicking of action of one anatomical area by another) which when coupled with synaesthesia (perceiving numerals as having colours) would, according to one neurophysiologist, lead to an understanding of Shakespeare's language. Such speculation is absurd. Let me explain why.

Obviously, he is referring to English. Any photographer will ask you to say 'Cheese' to elicit a smile before clicking the camera. But then the manner in which the lips have to be stretched to do this may have a different connotation in other languages.

In New Guinea alone there are 700 languages, each as different from the other as Chinese is from English. The shape the lips have to assume to represent joy in English may indicate grief in one of those languages!

Anthropologist Jared Diamond says that Neo-Melanesian, a sort of lingua franca of New Guinea, is as strict in its grammatical rules as is English. The word 'We' which in English is 'I plus you to whom I am speaking' is represented by Yumi and Mipela. When apologizing to a woman in her husband's presence for accidentally jostling her, he found to his embarrassment that in Neo-Melanesian the word 'Pushim' does not mean push but means 'have sexual intercourse with'. In Iyau, a single vowel has eight different meanings, including mother-in-law or beloved snake, depending on the pitch! It would be disastrous for a man to address his mother-in-law without this knowledge! Even distinguished linguists have not been able to fathom these pitch distinctions for years which Iyau children utter effortlessly.

If man has evolved from animals lacking human speech, then our language must have evolved with time along with organs like the pelvis, skull, etc. The intermediate language like stages, linking monkey grunts to advanced speech—is an enormous gulf which several Darwins and Newtons put together may find unbridgeable.

For all these reasons it would be ridiculous and even patronizing for any neuroscientist to even entertain a thought of analysing the brain of Shakespeare who excelled any other human being ever born, in the splendour of his imagination and the magnitude of his genius.

Let neuroscientists leave Shakespeare alone and stick to less ambitious but noble tasks like treating diseases of the brain!

43. *Poetry, the Greatest Creative Enterprise*

The other day I happened to come across the views of an eminent neurophysiologist, who speculated, towards the end of an address, that 'synaesthesia' a mingling of senses (i.e. perceiving numerals as having colour) and 'synkinesia' (mimicking of action of one anatomical area by another) which resonate with each other may have led to the evolution of language, and so a study of genetics will lead to an understanding of brain anatomy, and on to perceptual psychology and from there to Shakespeare's language.

In explaining the working of the brain, this very same neurophysiologist, had a few years ago, rejected the views of those who work on Artificial Intelligence and Neural Networks and who like to think of the brain as a computer. According to him the brain is a biological organ which evolved over aeons of time and developed its own style of functioning in a manner suited to 'evolutionary requirements' and not because a particular method was mathematically precise or aesthetically pleasing, i.e. nature chose the easiest way to get things done.

By the same token it may be desirable for neurophysiologist to avoid premature presumptions in explaining the 'leaps of imagination', that enable the extremely complex brains of poets to intuitively generate certain words and phrases. Would any one be able to say it better than Pope who wrote more than two and a half centuries ago.

> The sound must seem an echo to the sense:
> Soft is the strain when Zephyr gently blows,
> And the smooth stream in smoother number flows;
> But when loud surges lash the sounding shore
> The hoarse, rough verse should like the torrent roar.
> When Ajax strives some rock's vast weight to throw,
> The line too labours and the words move slow:
> Not so when swift Camilla scours the plane
> Flies O'er th' unbending Corn and skims along the main.

Leaving Shakespeare aside for a moment, let us take Tennyson's great onomatopoeic lines of excellence in *Morte d Arthur* in describing Sir Bedevere's march to the lake to get rid of the magic sword Excalibur.

By zig-zig paths and juts of pointed rock,
Came on the shining levels of the lake.

The closed syllables of the words in the first line create the image of a rough terrain, to cross every inch of which is an ordeal. The open syllables of the second line on the other hand create the image of the undisturbed surface of a calm lake. Tennyson did not frame his lines by picking words one by one. They just flowed out of his poetic brain.

It is one thing for a scientist to speculate about the manner in which, and the reason why, language evolved, but to say that a study of such biological processes would reveal the clue to Shakespeare's language is perhaps too tall a claim, at least at this stage of our knowledge of the brain. For there is certainly more at work in the 'mysterious brain that had conceived Hamlet and Macbeth, and the far-sighted vision that had plumbed the depths of life', than can be comprehended by any neuro-physiologiest! While conceding Nobel Laureate Peter Medawar's view-point that in terms of the fulfilment of 'declared intentions' science is incomparably the 'most successful enterprise' human beings have even engaged upon, we have to realize that poetry is incomparably the most 'creative enterprise' human beings ever engaged upon. And what is more, the question of declared intentions also does not arise in the case of poetry. Here, Shelley has the last word:

Like a Poet hidden
In the light of thought.
Singing hymns unbidden.
Till the world is wrought
To sympathy with hopes and fear it heeded not.

The punch is on 'Singing hymns unbidden
Till the world is wrought to sympathy!
i.e. the world has no option but to take notice of it!

And as one scientist himself had conceded, a scientist who discovers a law or unravels a secret of nature, just happens be the first to notice a phenomenon which is already present in nature, i.e. the word 'dis-covers' is misleading. It is just that he has seen it before others. If Einstein had not discovered relativity someone else would have done it. Minkowski, Michelson and Lorentz, were closing in—If Newton had not discovered Calculus someone else would have (Leibniz is credited with independently discovering it). If Crick and Watson had missed seeing the 'Double Helix' Linus Pauling would have seen it. But if

Shakespeare had not written *Othello* or *King Lear*, the world would never have had those plays! If Milton had not written *Paradise Lost* no one else would have!

For all these reasons it would be advisable for any scientist, however talented and brilliant to be extremely cautious when treading on unfamiliar grounds, e.g. dealing with men of infinitely superior intellectual calibre. I, for one, believe science would never be able to probe the working of the brain of William Shakespeare, the greatest genius mankind had ever produced.

44. *Shakespeare: A Dramatist who belongs to all Countries*

Every time I read Shakespeare, I come across some hitherto unnoticed aspect that serves only to reinforce my belief, that he has no equal in the entire annals of literature. This is not due to any special skill I possess, but because Shakespeare is like an ocean into which when you cast your net you always come up with something strange and new. This is how the realization suddenly dawned on me recently that he is 'International' in the sense he belongs to all lands. (Now, now, please do not point out that he left out this country or that. After all we are not dealing with a geography textbook!)

Let me explain what I mean. Sophocles never wrote a play more Greek than 'Timon of Athens'. One wonders whether Shakespeare was actually a citizen of Athens at the time of Particles. He heard with interest the speeches of the great Greek orators. Probably he could teach Demosthenes a thing or two about eloquence. His philosophy is more profound than that of Socrates; who else could have said:

> There is no darkness but ignorance!

He watched Socrates as he lay dying after having taken Hemlock. He observed Phidias carving the Parthenon and only on grave provocation, in a rare moment he wrote:

> Not marble nor the guided monuments
> Of princes shall outlive this powerful rhyme.

in one of those 154 great sonnets, which by themselves would have compelled us to regard him as the greatest of poets. Can any play be more Egyptian than 'Antony and Cleopatra'? One can see the Nile running through it. The Shadows of the Pyramids and the Sphinx fall over the play and they gaze into the desert forever though Shelley's 'Ozymandias' has already melted into the desert sands.

Can anyone say anything better about a woman than what he said about the Egyptian Queen, whose beauty, seductive charm and 'infinite variety' changed the course of the history of Rome? Italian passion sets the pages of 'Romeo and Juliet' aflame and young love bursts like a flower. 'Julius Caeser' makes old Rome rise like the Phoenix from its ashes and allows us to watch Antony stir up a quiet crowd, to 'rise and mutiny'. Some critics have tried to argue that Shakespeare's Roman crowds throw up their sweaty night caps—as English crowds do, but then we must remember that the Bard of Avon primarily wrote his plays for the theatre to entertain people drawn from various sections and such small mistakes have no serious implications. Secondly, Shakespeare frequently uses the word lass—a very typical word for an English girl. In fact, even in 'Antony and Cleopatra' we have!

> Now boast thee death, in thy possession lies
> A lass unparalleled.

What a way to refer to an Egyptian Queen!

But it appears that Shakespeare deliberately used that word to bring out the essential girlish aspect of Cleopatra.

The 'Winter's Tale' is set partly in Bohemia, 'Othello' in Venice and Cyprus, 'Measure for Measure' in Verona, and 'All's Well That Ends Well' in Paris, Florence and Marseilles. Space limitation does not permit me to quote many more instances but it would be appropriate to end this article by referring to 'The Tempest'.

'The Tempest' is set in a strange island which some critics feel is the 'New World'. Shakespeare seems to have diverted all his magic, music and mysticism from his earlier plays into a single magical drama 'The Tempest', which many consider his greatest achievement. In 'The Tempest', Shakespeare has reached a level beyond which human language cannot go. One wonders whether he had anticipated the phenomenal birth and growth of America—a country flowing with milk and honey!

45. Shakespeare's Symphony

Keats had said, 'Heard melodies are sweet, but those unheard sweeter'. Written melodies are the sweetest if the author happens to be Shakespeare. In some of his great lines there is music that excels the melodies of Mozart. By music, I mean an additional dimension to the blend of melody, harmony and rhythm, which, poetry alone has among the creative arts.

An appropriate analogy would be the movement of pieces in chess. The Rook moves only in straight lines, the Bishop diagonally but the Queen combines these, adding an extra dimension.

Limitations of space allow me to pick only a few flowers from an immense garden though all the great passages of Shakespeare teem with musical lines. I would like to invite the reader's attention to other passages also, which have this quality.

Take for example 'Julius Caesar' in which Cassius declares after the conspirators kill Caesar.

> How many ages hence
> Shall this our lofty scene be acted o'er
> In states unborn and accepts yet unknown!

What music!

or

Antony addressing Caesar's corpse in the same play

> O mighty Caesar! dost thou lie so low?
> Are all thy conquests, glories, triumphs, spoils,
> Shrunk to this little measure?

or

Juliet declaring her love for Romeo

> And when he shall die,
> Take him and cut him out in little stars.
> And he will make the face of heaven so fine
> That all the world will be in love with night.
> And pay no worship to the garish sun.

or

John of Gaunt describing England in Richard II

> This other Eden, demi-paradise
> This fortress built by nature for herself,
> Against infection and the hand the of war
> This happy breed of men, this little world
> This precious stone set in the Silver Sea.

and

Macbeth's realization of the futility of his actions.

> There's nothing serious in mortality
> All is but toys; renown and grace is dead
> The wine of life is drawn and the mere leese
> Is left this vault to brag of.

The music in the above lines has no parallel anywhere.

Can any one match the music in of Antony's words in 'Antony and Cleopatra'

> Let Rome in Tiber melt
> And the wide arch of the ranged empire fall
> Here is my space.

Referring to the passionate embraces of Cleopatra.

Or the words of an infuriated Lear in the last four lines of the greatest passage in all literature

> Turn all her mother's pains and benefits
> To laughter and contempt, that she may feel
> How Sharper than a serpent's tooth it is
> To have a thankless child.

This music is certainly not 'Heard Melody' though in the 'Two gentlemen of Verona' Shakespeare mentions every known musical term in his time. I am referring to music far more 'sublime, whose dwelling is the light of setting suns . . . And the blue sky'. Shakespeare's final verdict on existence delivered through propsero in the tempest

> I have bedimmed
> The noontide sun, call'd forth the mutinous winds
> And 'twixt the green sea and the azured vault
> Set roaring war: to the dread rattling thunder
> Have I given fire and rifted Jove's stout oak.
> With his own bolt: the strong-based promontory

have I made shake; and by the spurs pluck'd up.
The pine and cedar: graves at my command
Have wak'd their sleepers oped and let them forth.
By my so potent art. But this rough magic
I here abjure and, when I have required
Some heavenly music, which even now I do,
To work mine end upon their senses that.
This airy charm is for, I'll break my staff.
Bury it certain fathoms deep in the earth.
And deeper than did ever plummet sound
I'll drown my book.

Comparisons are odious, but Beethoven and Bach must bow their heads down to this great bard. I do not think that the world will ever have another creator of such 'heavenly music'.

46. *Shakespeare's Treatment of Feminine Beauty*

In Sanskrit and Greek drama, playwrights followed a conventions while describing feminine beauty—liberal use of simile, hyperbole and metaphor giving a detailed account of almost every organ. Women were classified into four categories, and only the most beautiful belonged to the first type, the 'Padmini', whose face was like the moon, eyes like the lotus, hair like dark clouds, breasts like a particular fruit or species of bird, an almost non-existent waist, a deep navel, so on and so forth. While such description was titillating a situation arose where the heroines of all the 'shringara prabhandas' (erotic epics) from 'Satyabhama' to 'Damayanti' possessed these attributes. Even allowing for poetic licence one wondered whether such anatomical description was necessary.

This is exactly where Shakespeare is different. Just a touch of literary flourish marked by subtlety, produced a greater effect than whole stanzas of an organ recital. The result—a procession of beautiful women; Viola, Rosalind, Juliet, Imogen and Katherine just to mention a few names which by themselves conjure up visions of Venus. Viola best illustrates Shakespeare's approach. Though Viola praises Silvia's beauty in the *Twelfth Night*, her own description of herself to the Duke, who believes she is a boy cannot be rivalled, for subtlety.

> She never told here love
> But let concealment, like a worm i' the bud,
> Feed on her damask cheek.

That word 'damask' gives Viola's cheek that touch of velvet pink or vivid rose with connotations of soft petals. Two other examples are the description of Desdemona's skin 'smooth as Monumental alabaster'. In *Othello* and Portia's hair silky soft as Gorden Ileece the *Merchant of Venus* respectively.

Rosalind in *As You Like It* combines girlish charm and feminine power and even makes it easy for Orlando to court her.

> Therefore Heaven nature charged
> That one body should be fill'd
> With all graces wide-enlarged:

Nature presently distill'd
Helen's cheek, but not her heart,
Cleopatra's majesty,
Atalanta's better part,
Sad Lucretia's modesty.
Thus Rosalind of many parts
By heavenly synod was devised.

Who else but Shakespeare could make Romeo say about Juliet.

Two of the fairest stars in all the heaven
Having some business, do entreat her eyes,
To twinkle in their spheres, till they return.
What if her eyes were there, they in her head?
The brightness of her cheek would shame those stars, . . .
O, that I were a glove upon that hand!
That I might touch the cheek!

Or make him say in grief:

Death, that hath suck'd the honey of thy breath,
Hath had no power yet upon thy beauty . . .
beaty's ensign yet
Is crimson in thy lips and on thy cheeks
And death's pale flag is not advanced there.

Could any one else match this portrait of Imogen in *Cymbeline*.

'Tis her breathing that
Perfumes the chamber thus: the flame o' the taper
Bows toward her, and would under-peep her lids,
To see the enclosed lights, now canopied
Under these windows, white and azure laced
With blue of heaven's own tinct.

or even better still

On her left breast
A mole cinque-spotted, like the crimson drops
I' the bottom of a cowslip.

or the magnificent manner in which Henry V who is in love with Katherine, the French princess, describes her

You have witchcraft in your lips, Kate:
There is more eloquence in a sugar touch of them than in the tongues
of the French Council; and they should soon persuade Harry of
England than a general petition of monarchs.

But it is in describing Cleopatra that Shakespeare excelled even his own unmatched felicity of expression.

Age cannot wither her
Nor custom stale
Her infinite variety:
Other women cloy
The appetites they feed;
She makes hungry
Where she most satisfies.

No other poet since the beginning of time nor in the future can ever pay such a tribute to a woman, compressing in two sentences, the two attributes that give a woman immense power, beauty that defies time, and sexual chemistry that keeps love play perpetually exciting, power that can change the course of history.

47. *Shakespeare and His Characters*

Shakespeare is considered the greatest genius ever born, because of his insight into every aspect of human behaviour and emotion—he packed his plays with 9,36,433 words out of which 27,870 are 'different words' (the highest vocabulary in history). The average person has only a speaking and writing vocabulary ranging from 2,000 to 3,000 words, and a recognition capacity of about 5,000 words. In great writers these figures grow to one and a half times or twice the number. Today our Modern English has two million words. Considering that Shakespeare did not even go to college you can imagine the magnitude of the intellect of the greatest genius mankind has ever known. He also possessed several mind-boggling qualities, which defy explanation. His greatest strength was imparting individuality and personality to a character, when other dramatists were satisfied with characters who became 'types'. This feature is particularly noticeable when there are two similar characters in a play. He creates this effect in such a manner that his characters behave like 'real people'. Shakespeare himself had reportedly said that if he had not killed Mercutio in *Romeo and Juliet*, Mercutio would have killed him!

As De Quincey had observed,

> In *Macbeth*, in order to gratify his own inordinate and teeming faculty of creation, Shakespeare has introduced two murders, and as usual in his hands, they are remarkably discriminated. (Macbeth and Lady Macbeth)

At the every beginning, on hearing that he had been made the 'Thane of Cawdor' as the witches had predicted, Macbeth gets ambitious to become the king, by killing Duncan. But Lady Macbeth who knows him observes,

> Yet to I fear thy nature;
> It is too full of the milk of human kindness;
> To catch the nearest way.

meaning Macbeth's timidity would come in this way. When Macbeth suddenly develops cold feet and says,

> We will proceed no further in this business;
> He has honoured me of late. . . .

She replies:

> Was the hope drunk
> Wherein you dressed yourself . . .
> Art thou afeard
> To be the same in thine own act and valor
> as thou art in desire.

and again

> I have given suck and know
> How tender 'tis to love the babe that milks me;
> I would while it were smiling in my face
> Have plucked my nipple from his boneless gums
> And dash'd the brains out, had I
> So sworn as you have done to this.

Even as Macbeth talks about a possible failure, her reply shocks Macbeth, who says,

> Bring forth men-children only
> For thy undaunted mettle shall compose
> Nothing but males.

After the deed is done, when Macbeth is trembling with fear and says,

> Wherefore could I do not pronounce Amen?
> I had most need of blessing and 'Amen'
> Stuck in my throat!

Lady Macbeth says,

> These deeds must not be thought
> After these ways; so it will make us mad!

and again

> Why worthy Thane,
> You do unbend your noble strength to think
> So brainsickly of things.

Throughout the play Macbeth is protected from emotional disintegration by his strong-willed and domineering wife, till she herself falls apart due to guilt towards the end.

In *Antony and Cleopatra* the Egyptian Queen has two attendants, Charmian and Iras. They are both close to her but Charmian comes out more prominently discussing with Cleopatra even her passion for Antony.

In *Julius Caesar* two tribunes Flavius and Marullus chide the crowds who had come to see Caesar. It is Marullus who sets the pace. Similarly during Antony's funeral speech, you can make out the first Plebeian easily by the way he takes charge of the gathering.

Thus Shakespeare's characters are not 'types', stuck to the Canvas or 'puppets' controlled by unseen strings.

They are real persons in whom good and evil mingle (unlike as in 'types') and who act on their own, once created. In the entire history of the world no other dramatist has achieved this.

It is precisely for this reason that you cannot take the views of Shakespeare's characters as his own, though in a few profound passages of some of his plays this extraordinarily marvellous man might have unguardedly let slip a few personal opinions—in the kaleidoscopically fluctuating moods of Hamlet, in the tempestuous agony of Lear, in the profound mysticism of prospero and in the terrifying verdict of a mentally shattered Macbeth who views life as a

> Tale told by an idiot.
> Full of sound and fury signifying nothing.

48. *Who Wrote the Shakespeare Plays?*

Whenever the subject of Shakespeare comes up someone is bound to say that Bacon or Marlowe wrote the plays, and not Shakespeare.

Now what difference does it make who wrote it. And in any case as Juliet herself said,

> What's in a name? That which we call a rose
> By any other name would smell as sweet.

Let us not speculate whether a part of one play or the whole of another play was written by Shakespeare or even that Shakespeare borrowed material from Plutach and Holinshed. The point is not who provided the canvas, paint and brush or the stone and chisel for Shakespeare. The point is that by not only being the greatest poet but also the greatest dramatist in history he combined harmoniously all the dimensions of creative art, producing unequalled paintings, carving, unrivalled statues and composing unmatched symphonies. He was Rembrandt, Phidias and Mozart, all three combined in one person. No wonder one famous art critic while discussing Rembrandt observed that Rembrandt representcd 'only one dimension' of Shakespeare!

Let us first discuss the 'Bacon theory'. The plays of Shakespeare reveal so much knowledge, wisdom and insight into human psychology that people who overrate the contribution of universities to genius would like to believe that Bacon, and not Shakespeare (who never went to college) must have been the real author. On the other hand the world is fortunate that the 'inordinate and teeming faculty of creation' of Shakespeare had not been cramped by 'formal education'. The magic of his 'own pen' produced powerful rhymes that will 'outlive' the marbles of Greece, the paintings of Michelangelo and the music of Beethoven.

Bacon had a regular education. But he was a 'scheming politician' and a time-server. As a judge he was corrupt. After sixty, he wrote some insipid poetry dedicated to George Herbert. One glance at those poems will convince you that this man could not have written the tempestuous passages in Macbeth or Lear.

Bacon regarded James-I as 'learned' though he was an ordinary man, who was also a stammering and trembling coward. Bacon claimed to be a scientist but held 'unscientific' views on various subjects and was ignorant of many genuine scientific developments. He erroneously believed in his own ability to make accurate observations on various phenomena, in order to explain which he put forth quixotic theories. According to Bacon, love was just something to be 'portrayed on the stage', but was not 'desirable' for real people. Do we need more proof to conclude that a man with such a perverse view of the greatest of human emotions could never have written Romeo and Juliet!

Bacon claimed the authorship of even every ordinary sentence he wrote, but not the plays of Shakespeare. Is it possible that such an intellectually dishonest person would not have claimed the greatest poetry of all time as his own?

Bacon's best can barely approach Shakespeare's ordinary passages (though there is no passage that can be so described) but Shakespeare's best is far beyond the reach of the greatest of poets, let alone Bacon.

The question of the authorship of Marlowe can be brushed aside more easily. No doubt, Marlowe wrote some good poetry, which earned the appreciation of Shakespeare himself. But there is an unbridgeable gap between the Himalayan peaks of Shakespeare poetry and the foot-hills of Marlowe's verses. The tribute paid by Ben Jonson, another great contemporary, to Shakespeare:

> how far thou didst our Lyle outshine
> Or sporting Kyd or Marlowe's mighty line

delivers the final verdict settling the controversy.

Shakespeare's poetry alone has that 'felicity of expression and rounded perfection' with its unmistakable stamp that can be recognized in every line he wrote.

Only once in the entire history of a planet does a star of such incandescent luminosity shine over it, bathing it in perpetual light, effulgence and glow. That star is Shakespeare.

49. Whither Shakespeare and Keats?

A few months ago when I wanted to buy a copy of the 'Oxford Book of English Prose'—a book I used to enjoy reading in my student days—I browsed through the literature section of all the major bookshops I usually visit in the twin cities (Hyderabad and Secunderabad). My search not only proved futile but I was sad, even shocked, to hear some of the replies I got. In one bookshop the salesgirl told me that they used to carry the book several months ago but that they had discontinued the sale of that book due to the lack of interest of the general reader in such books. In another shop, the owner himself, trying to be helpful, remarked that he would try to get it from Bombay or Delhi if I gave him the name of the author. I decided that there was no point in enlightening him about the fact that the book in question was an anthology and not the work of any single author!

Since I happened to visit Chennai recently I continued to look for a copy of the book in that city. To my dismay I found the same situation prevailing there also. The only course open for me now is to hope for the book to show up in one of the pavement shops that sell second-hand books, or ask a good friend going abroad to get it for me from the United States or the United Kingdom.

On the other hand, there was no dearth of books written by Johanna Lindsey or Daniel Steel not to mention Frederick Forsyth or Jeffrey Archer (the last two could at least be classified as 'reasonably good' in one particular category). My luck with the '*Sonnets of Shakespeare*' was slightly better (not as a part of the 'complete works' but as a separate volume); with great difficulty I could manage to get a copy from one shop, where it had been lying unsold for ages!

The realization suddenly dawned on me that ours is not an age of great poetry or lofty prose, in the sense the eighteenth and nineteenth centuries were in England. This is the age of pulp-fiction and cheap magazines and journals. No one gets inspired by reading 'Ode to a Nightingale' written by Keats, or 'The Rime of the Ancient Mariner' written by Coleridge. Nor does anyone want to be burdened with Dickens or Scott.

People have become addicted to thrillers containing violence and sexual exploits in abundant measure and so find novels that do not contain such material rather boring.

Television, video and cinema have to take a major share of the blame. If a person can spend three hours in an airconditioned hall watching exciting scenes of science fiction, battles fought out in space ships with laser guns or scenes containing steamy sex, how can you expect him or her to have the desire or patience to read 'Ivanhoe' in which all the action is confined to knights on horseback charging at each other with lances and all the sex that one can find is a modest kiss Ivanhoe gets from Rowena in the last page!

Unfortunately our schools and colleges do not have enlightened teachers who inculcate in students a love for lyrical poetry, or of eloquent prose. Our educational system also is geared so much towards success in examinations that there is no need or for that matter time to explain the greatness of Shakespeare!

What, therefore, is required is the creation of an intellectual environment which promotes a love of 'learning' for its own sake and stimulates the interest of students in Shelley's 'Ozymandias' or Gray's 'Elegy'. If and when this happens there is no need to explain the inherent value of great works of literature which have a perennial hold on man as compared to novels of ephemeral existence which have 'tumult' but no 'depth' to borrow an idiom from Wordsworth.

50. *Whither Indian English?*

During a visit to America a few years ago I had attended a party at a friend's house. The guests consisted of people of different nationalities, including an Italian, a Frenchman and a Venezuelan, all three of whom became the centre of attraction. The Italian was not exactly a Rudolf Valentino, but his pronunciation of words beginning or ending with 't' and 'd' made his conversation sound 'sexy' to the girls. The Frenchman was no Charles Boyer but was no less popular with the girls if only because there were echoes of Maurice Chevalier in his accent. The Venezuelan did not lag behind inasmuch as his sentences were sprinkled with words like '*Vestido*' or '*Bonita*'. No one was sure what the words meant but then who cares about meaning if the accent sounds exotic! Which incidentally brings me to the main subject of this essay, the manner in which English is spoken or written in various parts of the world.

At the outset, let me refer to the 'Style Guide' published by *The Economist*, arguably the best journal in the world in its genre. The 'Style Guide' justifiably claims that *The Economist* can hope to outwit its rivals on two scores—the quality of its analysis and the quality of its writing. The book is a serious but, at the same time, delightful thesis on English usage.

The second part of the book deals with what it refers to as 'American and British English'. In doing so, it accords formal recognition of American English probably having regard to the wealth, power and influence of the latter, considerations which do not seem to apply, for example, to Australia. But the real views of *The Economist* on American English are reflected in observations such as (a) 'Use Americanisms discriminatingly', (b) 'Many American words are unnecessarily long', e.g. automobile for car (c) 'Avoid using verb nouns or to adjective them, e.g. 'access files'. Advising that jargon should be avoided, the 'Style Guide' cites an example: 'We shall not launch the ground offensive until we have attrited the Republican Guard to the point when they no longer have an offensive capability' which according to it is the Pantagon's way of saying that the allies would not fight on the ground until they have killed so many Iraqis that the others would not attack. So also it draws attention to a press release from Israel. 'The US and Israel now possess the capability to conduct real time simulations with man in the loop for full-scale theatre missile defence architectures for the Middle East. In a classic example of matchless British humour, the 'Style Guide' remarks that the meaning of the sentence 'remains unclear'. So also it looks down upon long words as being redundant, e.g. one American Ambassador to Britain discovered this after describing his first expressions of his new home as 'necessitating a degree of refurbishment'. It discourages the use of 'ugly and over-used expressions' such as bottomline (a favourite word of our cousins in America), recommends avoiding the use of the word plane for Airplane unless a surface or tool actually flies! To sum up, the 'Style Guide' while indicating its preference for Telephone to phone and chips to French Fries grudgingly accepts that American English is here to stay and reluctantly admits that Americanisms have passed into the English language.

Now let us take a look at the state of English in our country, which has had an association of more than 200 years with that language. We have novelists, writers and journalists famous the world over. English is spoken and understood even in the remotest corners of the country. Hundreds of newspapers, journals and books are produced in English on almost every subject. To cite an example they all about a dozen magazines on films and another dozen on sports.

Despite all this, most Indians do have a sort of complex with respect to English. No doubt an ability to write good English or speak fluently is to be admired. But a tendency to regard those who lack such skills as old fashioned, as is noticeable in our country, has to be discouraged. No German or Japanese would feel awkward on account of an inability to speak good English. He has a natural attitude of taking such a limitation in his stride. Then why should we have contempt for those of our countrymen who have not had the opportunity to become proficient in English? As long as Americans retain 'rain check', 'couch potato', 'momentarily depart', 'phoney', 'fun guy' and 'a bunch of crap' is there really any need for us to give up 'pindrop silence', 'neck out', 'issueless', 'co-son-in-law', 'cooling glasses' and 'cousin-brother'?

51. *Of Poets and Scientists*

When the great French mathematician Laplace lay dying, he was surrounded by all his children, grandchildren, and even great grandchildren. They tried to console him saying that he had achieved more than millions of others, obviously referring to his mathematical papers. The mathematician had one last glance at all his family members, and with tear-stained eyes brushed aside those papers, saying that they were not the 'important' things in life. 'What then?' they asked in amazement. Fighting for one last breath he answered 'love'.

Noble as the declaration was, the point is that Laplace for all his mathematical genius could realise this only just before he died—an emotion all poets know from an early age intuitively. Indeed death is one of the common themes of poetry. Poets do write about other emotions also, a poem to a sweetheart; a graphic description of a battle or the exploits of a great warrior like Ulysses but even in such poetry there are flashes of insight into mortality. There is something about the way a poet says about such things, that makes the reader wish that he had written those lines.

Scientists might argue, not without some justification, that their discoveries and inventions have improved the quality of man's life on this planet and that we would have still been in the dark ages without science. But then Omar Khayyam would reply . . .

> Here with a Loaf of Bread beneath the Bough,
> A Flask of Wine, A Book of Verse—and Thou
> Beside me singing in the Wilderness—
> This Wilderness were Paradise enow.

Richard Lovelace, even from prison could say about liberty.

> Stone walls do not a prison make.
> Nor iron bars a cage
> Minds innocent and quiet take
> That for a hermitage:
> If I have freedom in my love
> And in my soul am free
> Angels alone that soar above,
> Enjoy such liberty.

Mozart was quite happy without an electric guitar or a bush sound system. The basic ingredients required to constitute happiness are few and free, available everywhere. Milton did not have to go Disney Land to get excitement. But his 'Paradise Lost' is greater than all the theme parks put together.

The combined ages of Byron, Shelley and Keats before they died was just about 90 years but within that period they produced poetry that will last till the end of time.

Scientists constantly improve upon the discoveries made earlier. Newton himself admitted that he had been able to see 'farther' than most others, because he stood on the shoulders of giants. Poets don't have to do that. They are not interested in seeing farther than most others!

If a scientific truth is not discovered by X, Y will discover it sooner or later. In fact, at any given point of time hundreds of people might be working on a problem. On gets at the solution by luck, or an early start, or some other factor. He is supposed to have 'discovered' it. Newton and Leibniz independently discovered calculus. If Einstein had not discovered relativity, Lorentz or Michelson or Minkowski would have done it. If Crick and Watson had missed seeing the 'Double Helix', Pauling or Chargoff would have recognised it. Nor would a poet gloat over somebody's failure to reach the goal first, as Crick and Watson had done. Poets are preoccupied with nobler things.

Poets and scientists have an entirely different approach to life. A poet 'loves' his sweetheart. A scientist 'lusts' after a woman. A poet is compassionate, most scientists are cold and calculating at least the few I know well. 'Idealism' motivates a poet. It is 'ambition' that motivates a scientist. A scientist will do anything however unethical to get his paper published. A poet lives in obscurity 'hidden in the light of thought' not bothering about recognition.

Why has such a situation arisen ? After all, scientists being extraordinarily gifted persons, one would have expected them to go about their work for the sheer thrill of discovery not to mention the celebrity status conferred on them by virtue of the prizes won and media propaganda. Probably the nature and rules of the game themselves promote competition that degenerates into unhealthy rivalry and clash of egos. On the other hand, great as the achievements of science have been, Shakespeare and Milton, Valmiki and Kalidasa can never lose their perennial hold on man and the world is compelled to take notice of their work to protect the moral fabric of civilization.

52. *Not Every One is a Genius*

Gray, in his 'Elegy', arguably the most famous poem in English, observed that among the buried, there might be some 'mute inglorious Milton' who had no opportunity to reveal his genius, just as undiscovered gems on the ocean floor or fragrant flowers in the desert.

Bertrand Russel had shattered the comfortable doctrine that genius will always make its way despite 'persecution' of young talent like, the misconception that murder will out. He rightly argues that obviously all the murders we know of have been discovered but there must be many which have not been heard of. Likewise, the geniuses we know of have had circumstances in their favour, but there may be innumerable others who succumbed (due to their own timidity) to a domineering father, and taken up mundane careers. The father's financial insecurity, during his own childhood, had perhaps forced him to suppress the boy's talent. In many families due to such factors the elder son, though brighter than his younger brother, might not have been bold enough to rebel against paternal tyranny and pursue a career of his own choice, say literature, and given up his idealism. By the time the younger son had reached adulthood the father himself would have acquired some financial security and generous attitude allowing the younger boy to pursue his chosen career, even providing active support.

The term 'genius' itself is loosely used, particularly in our country, whatever the degree of talent, to lakhs of people pursuing various disciplines. Mere ability to produce a shapeless figure, which is a cross between a Mogdialini and a Dali, a skill to write leftist-oriented articles on currently topical themes of social injustice, under the head 'investigative journalism' particularly in a book form (it is considered a mark of 'scientific manhood' to study, and write about 'rural poverty' and expose the exploitation of the down-trodden: a view shared by some bureaucrats who regard themselves intellectual), a cleverness to produce poetry that seems to convey a certain idea but actually means something else, a moderate degree of proficiency that secures a thesis in one of the sciences or mathematics and a professorial chair, particularly in America (indeed there are thousands of them there) or making a simple technological device of limited application, will not qualify a person to be called a genius. There are millions of people like this all over the world who can at best be classified as very bright. There are countless number of others, whose significantly higher achievements and awards would earn them only a classification of 'brilliant'. Even a fellowship of the Royal Society may not be enough by itself, a Nobel Laureate may just make it, but in that 'very wide spectrum' there is a huge gulf between men like Einstein, Bohr, Dirac and Rutherford, who revolutionized physics and someone whose contribution was limited to being an 'ordinary member' of a team making a discovery.

Hence, we must treat the term 'genius' with respect. They are born very rarely, perhaps, a hundred of them in every century. Against such a scenario, just imagine the stature of 'myriad-minded' Shakespeare equated by Coleridge to 'five thousand Newtons'. From that firmament, where Shakespeare dwells apart in solitary unrivalled splendour as the brightest star, when you look down in this earth, and see those who strut about pompously, either in a laboratory or a university corridor, and referring to themselves as geniuses on the basis of some findings of no great significance, would it not look annoying, pathetic and even ridiculous.

53. *Two View Points on the Human Condition*

When Gray wrote that 'the paths of glory lead but to the grave' he was echoing the general view of poets who more than any other category of persons are pre-occupied with the ephemeral nature of human existence and regard all the 'glories of our blood and state' as 'shadows not substantial things'. This is not to belittle the triumphs of others, like let us say scientists, who unravel nature's secrets, and incidentally create technology that is of benefit to mankind. It is just that the purpose of science itself imposes limitations on its ability to solve certain issues. Science is concerned with the 'how' of things and not the 'why'. Most scientists themselves know this inherent restriction, and are not perturbed about it, just as the driver of a railway engine would not sit and worry about his engine not being able to fly. Of course, they ask persons putting such questions to turn to philosophers or poets for 'solace' if not 'answers'. If such an advice is 'sincere' there is no objection but scientists will have to be cautioned against any hint of a patronising suggestions that they are superior to anyone else. The popular image of an absent-minded scientist fumbling over test-tubes, not remembering whether he had his lunch, let alone not finding way to his house, is totally without justification. On the contrary, the history of science is replete with examples of one scientist claiming credit for the work of another, a team claiming to have published papers before another or even scientists alienating blood-brothers for real estate; on the contrary, poets even at an early age are obsessed with death and existence and keep brooding and hovering around graveyards like Gray, or staring at the ocean like Byron. To a scientist death is a mere statistical event occurring every day in a hospital or a house. Their greatest idea of beauty also is an equation or a metal dissolving in an acid, and not the beauty of a flower or the stellar firmament. As against this let us see what young Byron wrote in 'The Prisoner of Chillon'.

> Oh! God! it is fearful thing
> To see the human soul take wing
> In any shape, in any mood
> I've seen it on the breaking ocean

strive with a convulsive motion
I've seen the sick and ghastly bed
of sin delirious with its dread.

Which brings out the full pathos and horror of death.

Between the ages of 25 and 40 no scientist would think of death. He will be 'ambitious', wanting to discover something and win prizes, whereas a Keats or a Shirley would be troubled by thoughts of mortality. In moments of triumph scientists pat each other on their backs, play bongo drums, or childishly get out of a tub or run down a street to announce success! The poet William Cullen Byrant was only 27 when he wrote:

So live, that when the summons come to join.
The innumerable caravan, which moves
To that mysterious realm, where each shall take
His chamber in the silent halls of death,
Thou go not, like the quarry-slave at night,
Scourged to his dungeon, but, sustained and soothed
By an unfaltering trust, approached thy grave
Like one who wraps the drapery of his couch.
About him, and lies down to pleasant dreams.

Why then do we have to go as far as Keats, Milton or the greatest of them all 'incomparable' Shakespeare.

The following story sums up what I have stated and would make a good poem, but to a scientist it may not make much sense. In 1989 in a small town in America the elder of two brothers was dying of cancer.

He wanted to have a Christmas party, as had been their custom every year. The party went off with Dickensian joviality, but when all the guests had departed, came the heart-rending realisation, that so many friends of long years and decades would never be seen again, not in the next year, not ever. This is the most tragic aspect of the human condition, the frightening thought of everlasting separation of loved ones, friends of long years of association, who will never ever meet again, disappearing into the mists of time, making a mockery of human experience—an emotion beyond the mental horizon of a scientist but about which only poets feel intensely and also intuitively. And this to me represents the basic difference between poets and any one else—let alone scientist!

PART V

SPORTS, PASTIME AND OTHER MATTERS

54. *Bradman's Team*

Several months ago, one day like any other cricket aficionado I grabbed the sports section of the papers with great enthusiasm when I heard about a dream team having been chosen by the Don (Needless to mention that I practically worship the Don and regard him the 'greatest sportsman' of all time, i.e. not just as a cricketer but greater than Pele in football and Michael Jordan in baseball notwithstanding the fact that such comparisons are considered irrational). But I was not only not prepared for the great anticlimax that greeted my eyes but was quite surprised and even shocked to notice the composition of the team. The great man appeared to have made only two mistakes in his entire career. His first mistake was to have been bowled by Hollies for a zero just when he needed four runs to get an average of one hundred in Test Cricket. (I can think of at least one cricketer whose passion for records is so great, that he would have stayed on for two hours at the crease just to get those four runs, or at least announced, he was not going to retire till he achieved the magic mark never mind he could never have achieved such an average even in his dreams!)

Now let us have a look at several flaws that seem to have crept in, partly because no one, not even the Don, can just pick eleven stars in a galaxy, partly because of certain personal prejudices which even he himself had not been free from, and partly because of his sense of misplaced generosity at his rather advanced age. How can one otherwise justify his exclusion of Hammond (putting him as the twelfth man is adding insult to injury!), Hutton, Hobbs and Ponsford and the inclusion of Arthur Morris? I am afraid that many people are not aware that Bradman and Hammond did not exactly like each other, as clearly outlined in the book 'Number one' by Simon Wilde. So also the omission of Larwood cannot be accepted. Bradman in his own book admits that Larwood used to bowl with 'exceptional speed'. Perhaps memories of the controversial 'bodyline' era had made Bradman reluctant to include Larwood, though he himself had regarded Larwood as the fastest bowler the game had ever known. Can any one afford to ignore Jim Laker, the greatest off spinner of all times whose feat of taking 19 wickets in a test can never be repeated, just as Bradman's batting average of 99.94? Everton Weekes of the West Indies is another great batsman who cannot be omitted from any list. That short man from the Caribbean taught a whole generation of bowlers what 'cutting' was all about. So also in one particular era Viv Richards tore apart all the opposition bowling with ease, piling up runs with amazing speed. The skill, power and range of strokes of Barry Richard, an extremely talented batsman, have obviously earned him a place in this dream team. Similarly, Tendulkar, who has shown great promise with technique, mastery over stroke play, and fast run-getting ability, which are characteristics of all the greatest batsmen, should be there though he would necessarily have to score a few double centuries failing which it would remain a serious blot on his career. By the same token the Don should have included in his dream team, the great Neil Harvey whose aggression and wristy strokes produced great scores that had thrilled all cricket lovers. Again, the non-inclusion of all-rounders of the calibre of Keith Miller and Ian Botham would come as a surprise to everyone. In their day they dominated the field irrespective of whether they were batting or bowling. Wicket-keeper Knott or Evans in addition to Don Tallon must find a place in the team.

So what do we conclude? It is impossible to pick only eleven names in a game that has so many great players, who have left their footprints on the sands of many cricket fields. Nor can we pick a team of fifty for obvious reasons. So let us have a team of twenty-two: Bradman, Hammond, Hobbs, Hutton, Sobers, Weekes, Ponsford, Miller, Botham, Larwood, O'Rielly, Grimmett, Laker, Bedser, Evans (or Knott), Tallon, Viv Richards, Lindwall, Lilee, Harvey, Barry Richards and Tendulkar. I am sure this would be a composition that would have met even the Don's approval.

55. *Cricket 'Now' and 'Then'* (1)

One of the ingredients in the enjoyment of any sport is the endless arguments that takes place about the comparative merits of the players. Only in athletics is it possible to say that the present day athletes are better than their predecessors, as the passage of time as well as the potential of human physiology allow for such improvements, reflected as records being broken except in some isolated cases like that of Jesse Owens; for a factor known as relative performance still keeps Owens ahead of Carl Lewis despite the former's record having been bettered.

But in respect of present day cricket the players look larger than life due to media propaganda and also because, human psychology being what it is, this generation would like to believe that contemporary cricketers are the best ever. The images of better dressed cricketers appear everyday on the TV screen and in glossy magazines.

They are seen with glamour queens and they endorse consumer products ranging from cars to soft drinks, which earn them millions of rupees. Cricket aficionados of today are indifferent to the legends of yesteryears and react to the mention of their names with a patronizing grin which seems to imply that those so-called 'greats' probably batted on easy pitches or perhaps faced bowling not of the same hostility as present batsmen encounter and that only a sense of nostalgia attributes to them a stature they really did not possess.

Venkata Narasimham, while thanking the Wisden panel in nominating the top fifty cricketers of the last century, expresses similar views.

While appreciating the efforts of the panel in nominating them he also observes that new followers of the game generally seem to know only the shorter version of the game and are not sufficiently informed of the real cricket greats. Everyone in the panel of 100 experts drawn from different countries had only one name in common which was that of the Don.

In Wisden's list, Sobers is rated second. Gavaskar lands a place at no. 12 and Tendulkar is ranked no. 17. Narasimham says that this verdict puts 'all the notions, endless comparisons of all and sundry with Bradman, where it really belongs . . . in the "garbage bin". The ludicrous claim of some people that Tendulkar is even better than the

"Don" may be easily dismissed as a joke, only that no one is laughing.' But of late Tendulkar has been piling up records e.g. crossing the 10,000 runs mark as well as Bradman's twenty-nine centuries. He has age and frequency of more test matches on his side. But he is yet to score a single double century and his run average not impressive (as against Bradman's double centuries, two triple centuries and run average of 99.94!).

Then how do we go about deciding the who and why of the best of cricket. In his rather delightfully written book 'Between The Wickets' Surjit Bhalla carries out an extremely complicated exercise involving several variables. He uses a method of standardization, bringing all teams of all countries to a common ground, and making suitable adjustments for pitch conditions, weather, strength of either side bowling as well as batting, devising weightage and indicators whenever necessary. His argument gains credibility as he steers clears of preconceived notions and analyses all factors objectively.

He develops a theory of weight index number for batsmen as well as bowlers whose veracity is irrefutable. What would come as a shock to all cricket enthusiasts in this country is that in the table listing the top fifty batsmen of all time there is no present day Indian batsman. In fact, only two figure in the list: Hazare at no. 31 with a win figure of 32 and Gavaskar at no. 33 with a win figure of 34. However nobody would deny that Tendulkar has already earned for himself a place in that list well above Hazare and Gavaskar. Not surprisingly, Bradman comes first with a win figure of 952. With Hobbs (832), Headlay (828) and Weekes occupying the second, third, and fourth places. Other all-time greats appear on the list, e.g. Hutton (716), Sobers (693), Harvey (684), Hammond (666), Border (654), and Lloyd (648) way above our two batsmen. So do G.S. Chappel (661) and Worrell (639). To quote Bhalla 'what is interesting is not that Bradman is the best all-time batsman, but the fact that he dominates other players in almost every category possible or imaginary; what is interesting is that no amount of adjustments or juggling or weighing can change Bradman's occupancy of his rightful chair. And again, as the British mathematician Hardy said, Bradman is a whole class above any batsman who ever lived; if Archimedes, Newton and Gauss remain in the Hobbs class, I have to admit the possibility of a class above them which I find difficult to imagine.

56. Cricket 'Now' and 'Then' (2)

The opinions of other great cricketers vindicate the results of Surjit Bhalla as well as the later conclusions of the Wisden panel. Years ago when Vijay Merchant was asked his views about cricket, he remarked with a mischievous twinkle in his eyes that we do not have a single batsman today like someone in his era who scored a century before lunch, another before tea, and the third century before stumps were drawn. He was of course referring to Don Bradman.

Lala says he was fortunate to have walked with the Don for toss. He quotes Jardine as having confessed that it was not easy to set the field for the Don and that he had bowled to great batsmen like Hammond, Hutton and Compton. But it was different when the Don strode to the crease. Reacting to a remark that Bradman never played one-day cricket, Lala described it as a 'silly remark'. 'I wish he had played one-day cricket. Cricket fans would have seen a level of batsmanship unknown to them! Such was Bradman's mastery that even test cricket was one-day cricket for him. So please don't insult the Don by making silly comparisons.'

Really then there is no need to quote the views of everyone. All of them are unanimous in their verdict. Bradman bestrides the cricket world like a colossus. What magnificent figures they are—(a) a test average of 99.94. He needed only four runs to make it hundred. But he was ironically bowled for zero; (The next best average is only 65.) (b) 29 hundreds in 58 innings. Ten of these were double centuries. One double century was 299. Two were triple centuries; (c) Most runs in a series, that is, 974 in 7 innings; (d) Fastest 2000, 3000, 4000, 5000 and 6000 runs; (e) Six centuries in six consecutive innings; (f) There was no shot he could not play, but the pull was his favourite. He could even pull a ball going wide off the off stump; (g) Wore no headguard or other protection even against the great Larwood who was hurling a blood red missile at him in the infamous Bodyline series. Even then developed a strategy to get an impressive average, including a century in one innings; (h) He could see the ball earlier than any other batsman; (i) A century in every third innings.

What justification do we have then to hastily refer to any rising star, however impressive, as the Don, the only player to have a definite article before his name. The players of today with unlimited access to big money, with all its sordid ramifications as we are witnessing now, the blind adoration of millions of fans who confuse patriotism with admiration or affection, sought after by gorgeous girls with little knowledge of the game, heavily padded and protected before going to bat as though going to battle, being retained in the team despite dismal performances have brought this 'gentleman's game' to ignominy, shame and disrepute.

It is no mere nostalgia that makes us recollect memories of the kind of excellence the game may not see again—the devastating pull of Don Bradman, the murderous hook of Walter Hammond, the punishing cover drive of Viv Richards, and the aggressive square cut of Everton Weekes, just to name a few.

What was the secret of their success? Discipline, dedication, devotion, a passion for perfection, humility in respect of their own talent, a genuine admiration for their rivals, and above all a certain respect for the values and principles that represent the game of cricket which place team, country and sportsmanship above self !

57. *How Reliable are Opinion Polls?*

Several months ago I had written an article entitled 'Cricket' 'now' and 'then' and a little later another on 'Bradman's team'. I had also written one 'on movies and actors today'. I must confess that nostalgia had influenced my views to a certain extent. But verdicts given in several authoritative books written by knowledgeable persons on the basis of statistical data (in respect of cricket) and time-honoured traits intuitively and universally regarded as essential for an actor to be referred to as 'great' had conveyed a moral sanction to my opinions.

In this connection I would like to invite the attention of the general reader to the so called 'polls' held from time to time in various parts of the world by various organizations, which announce the name of the 'winner' in almost every field of human activity with an air of 'finality'.

A few months ago, all Indians had been delighted to hear the verdict of the 'BBC' that Amitabh Bachchan was most popular (or whatever) actor of all time, and that he had even been immortalized in wax in Madame Tussaud's in London (another new item appeared on 17 Dec about a poll result showing Robert de Niro as the greatest actor of all time). I am also a great fan of Amitabh and have seen most of his films. I have watched with interest his show 'Kaun Banega Crorepati' on television, which he conducted with style and dignity. But I am afraid that this is where our admiration for the man must stop. Period. To get over-excited by our own enthusiasm and patriotism and take the result of some isolated poll, conducted under circumstances we are not aware of as 'Gospel truth', merely because it suits us would be erroneous. The ability of a good tennis player must be judged by his performance at Wimbledon or Flushing Meadows over a period of time—not the members of the Secunderabad club or an opinion poll conducted in Jubilee Hills or Begumpet. The same is the case with de Niro. No doubt he is one of the best actors today. But I doubt whether he can even be put in the class of Antony Hopkins who is considered by many as the great living actor. In a list of the greatest actors of all time prepared by any recognized 'authority' on movies anywhere, Sir Lawrence Oliver would be at the top along with Sir John Greigud and Sir Ralph Richardson (the famous British trio). They will be followed closely by Alice Guinness, Ronal Colman, Spencer Tracy, Frederick March, Richard Harris, Charles Boyer, Charles Laughton, etc. Oliver's position as the greatest actor of the twentieth century is unquestioned and his stature as a colossus is acknowledged by no less a person than our own Nasiruddin Shah, a great actor himself, a sentiment echoed by even Spencer Tracy and Charleton Heston. In fact Spencer Tracy referred to Olivier as 'the greatest of them all'. The order of greatness of the other actors can perhaps be shuffled about.

Let us now come to cricket. Just when we had been recovering from the shock of the great Don having made the mistake of excluding Walter Hammond, Neil Harvey, Harold Larwood and Jim Laker from his dream team, Ian has came with a list of 100 cricketers that excludes the great Don himself! Of course, Botham justified his selection by stating that he had named only players he had been associated with. If that were to be the case, every player can come out with a list of his own.

On the other hand, I would have expected Botham, one of the 'greatest all-rounders' cricket has even known, not to commit such a 'grievous fault'. It would have been perhaps better for Botham not to have come out with such a book that does not pay homage to the Don, notwithstanding his criteria for making the choice!

58. On Movies and Actors Today

Like in cricket or any other sport, cinema is a field in which endless animated discussions enhance our appreciation of the experience. Everyone has their favourite actor or actress and no amount of evidence presented to the contrary would persuade them to revise their opinion. In a sense, sports enthusiasts have an advantage as ranking is always related to performance which is usually measurable with mathematical accuracy; thus there will never be any doubt regarding Bradman's supremacy since he comes out on top whatever be the yardstick. In acting, however, such yardsticks are not available and the choice of the best actor or best actress cannot be precise or exact and the panel making the choice will invariably be accused of some lack of objectivity. Under these circumstances, how do we pick the best?

But then here also there are certain universal traits intuitively recognized by all to be necessarily found in a great actor, whatever the society or country. These include a capacity to be realistic so as to merge with the character portrayed; an ability to convey some of the basic emotions like anger, hatred, love, sympathy, greed and jealousy without being accused of overacting; a degree of eloquence or rhetoric when it is called for in a character; a capacity to improvise in a natural manner, should the conditions of the scene demand it; a willingness to resist the urge to push the other actors into the background even if the actor in question has only a brief appearance as a guest and the hero is a novice or of comparatively lesser stature. Example: Lawrence Olivier who acts as a Roman nobleman in *Spartacus* merges with the character so completely that he does not allow Kirk Douglas to be overawed; John Gielgud the valet of Richard Wildmark in *Murder in the Orient Express* behaves like a typical English valet and allows Wildmark full freedom!

There is also an element of what is called style, which cannot be defined but is easily recognizable. When several actors play a similar kind of role you can easily pick the one who has the charisma. By style we do not mean being ostentation; it is a combination of personality, presence, elegance and articulation.

Let us take James Bond, for instance. Five actors have so far played the part. But this quality is present only in Sean Connery in the way he walks or talks or holds his gun, checks out of his room, wears his suit, or delivers one-liners. It is not just one-liners alone. All the actors utter them. But Sean Connery says them in a certain manner which others don't. When he was awarded an honorary Oscar for his contribution to the cinema he was requested to speak. He introduced himself as 'My name is Connery—Sean Connery' bringing the house down with a long ovation by echoing the BOND delivery, famous all over the world for the right pause!

Again, so many actors play action roles—Stallone, Willis, Seagal, Banderas, Van Damme, Brosnan, Ford, Cage, Travolta and Gibson but they do not have the Sean Connery style. In the movie *Rock*, he totally eclipses Nicholas Cage.

Modern cinema concentrates more on cinematography, special effects portraying huge disasters or science fiction in which the individual actor has no role to play—thus cannot be blamed. By the very nature of their production contemporary movies do not give any chance to an actor to show his brilliance (here and there, one may come across a Robert De Niro or an Anthony Hopkins, but they are exceptions.) Technology dominates cinema like never before. Leonardo de Caprio sinks with the '*Titanic*'.

What did the actors of the early 1930s to the 1960s possess which present day actors either do not possess or do not have a chance to display. With very little help from early cameras, poor sound equipment, studios with rudimentary facilities and improvised temporary sets, those actors had to rely solely on their own acting ability, personality, articulation and style. Yet another factor was their wide experience of theatre, particularly Shakespeare and other great dramatists. See them again at a glance, these remarkable people: Lawrence Olivier was the greatest actor of the twentieth century uttering the most famous soliloquy of all times: 'To be or not to be' in *Hamlet*; John Gielgud, as he brings out all the shock and agony of Julius Caesar after being stabbed in the senate by his dearest friend Brutus; Richard Johnson spitting venom in asking Brutus 'why man he doth bestride the narrow world like a Colossus', while referring to Julius Ceasar; in the movie *Cromwell* Richard Harris explaining in a husky voice that 'the King is not England and England is not the King'; a dying Cleopatra (Vivien Leigh) addressing her real husband (Lawrence Olivier) 'Husband I come' though in the play itself he is only her lover (Antony); and Bette Davis as Elizabeth concealing her attraction for Essex even as she orders his execution in *Mary Queen of Scots*.

Long before Richard Gere courted Julia Roberts in *Pretty Women* or Seagal took on the hijackers in *Under Seige,* dashing Errol Flynn could swashbuckle and kiss his way to any woman's heart; Debonair Clark Gable could make Vivien Leigh's heart flutter with the look he gave from the bottom of the stairs in *Gone with the Wind* Handsome Tyronne Power could make Rita Hayworth swoon with his charm in *Blood and Sand* and fearless tall and lanky . . . Gary Cooper could walk down the main street in High noon to save a small western town.

Lawrence Olivier uttering the four fold 'no' in *Lear* with agony, Guinness asking for protection from the cold to prevent people from thinking that he was shivering out of fear of death, Gielgud saying 'Yon Cassius has a lean and hungry look. He thinks too many such men are dangerous'. This really is acting at its best—a level beyond which it is impossible for human ability to go.

Even Hollywood does not need or have such actors any more. Their genius lies in old films in the archives, preserved as the conscience and memories of a golden age when style, acting ability and romance defined the greatness of a movie. There is an anecdotic about Lawrence Olivier and Dustin Hoffman who were paired together in the *Marathon Man*. While some of the scenes were being shot, Dustin Hoffman himself considered to be a great actor tried all kinds of antics to put life into the character he played. He performed exercises, ran till he got exhausted, left the beard unshaven, etc. Olivier was apparently sitting in a corner watching all this with an amused grin. The director was also assisting Dustin Hoffman to get the best out of him. (No director has the capacity or courage to direct Lawrence Olivier!) At last a desperate Hoffman turned to Olivier and asked him what more he had to do to achieve perfection. 'Just act' said Olivier without even a hint of arrogance. Here was an Olivier. When comes such another?

59. Bollywood and Tollywood

Most Indian movies (whether in Telugu, Tamil, Hindi or any other language) are referred to as 'family entertainers' or 'social films', two terms which are broadly supposed to mean that all the members of the family can enjoy watching them together. There are fights for the kids, sex and passion for the youth depicted as 'duets'—a vertical expression of a horizontal desire in which the hero and heroine chase each other in gardens, all over the world.

There is a 'dream sequence' in which the 'indifferent' heroine falls accidentally into the hero's arms, suddenly develops love, clutches the pillow to her bosom at night on her bed, and imagines a duet. There is a gossip and plenty of melodrama for the elders, in which the main characters pontificate on various values. (There is also a scene where 50 girls in similar diaphanous costumes and a few boys sing songs with suggestive words along with the heroine.)

The story is usually a theme involving the interaction between the members of one family with those of another with others causing complications. Of special importance is the villain who entertains lustful thoughts for the heroine, not to mention other women, but he also hates the hero. He gets more opportunities for physical contact with the heroine; whereas the hero has to maintain a constant distance of six feet except perhaps in one or two scenes in which he has a chance to rest his head on the heroine's lap or clasp her to his bosom. The hero is the ideal son, ideal husband, and also an ideal brother! But he has double-standards because he cannot stand the idea of his sister being courted by anybody. By chance if he happens to notice them in a park he develops a homicidal fury. Of course, the sister always 'throws up'—a sign of pregnancy but the heroine apparently has been taking sufficient precautions!

If the hero is a trade union leader, the heroine is the superintendent of police. But if he happens to be the head of the police force, she is the defence lawyer. The grandfather is the judge. As fast as court procedure is concerned, anybody can intervene at any time, and the Evidence Act is conveniently ignored. Whether the hero is a police chief or a doctor or a trade union leader he is unrivalled in Kung Fu, having been trained probably by Bruce Lee, and but then what is comical is that while he despatches 40 of the villain's assistants in four minutes, he takes 40 minutes to tackle the limping, one-eyed villain in the last scene, after himself coming out of the jaws of death 20 times! (Even if the villain is getting away in Jeep, our hero in a bullock-cart can catch up with him!)

There are other interesting features. Everyone, including the grandmother, can handle a revolver with accuracy of a James Bond, notwithstanding the fact that the revolver by virtue of the small distance that the bullet has to travel in the barrel is the most difficult weapon to use.

There is practically no film without a rape; the victim is usually the hero's sister or a blind girl; in either case the rapist is compelled to marry the girl in a strange form of justice. And the heroine, on being accused of infidelity walks towards 'nowhere in particular' in between the tracks of a rail-road or jumps into a river from a bridge only to be rescued by a priest!

Cobras are used for all sorts of purposes; often the heroine is a cobra who disappears at night and returns before the hero wakes up in time to give him tea.

There is also another feature present practically in every film—twins being separated at birth by the villain or accident and reunited in the last scene in which one of them has to die for the benefit of the heroine, unless she also has a twin.

The last scene is chaos with so many people fighting so many others in so many places and in so many ways that one tends to lose track of things. Babies are thrown in the air but just saved in time. Out of this chaos the hero emerges victorious, saves the heroine, her mother, his mother, etc.

All the family members gather at one place distributing sweets. All is well that ends well. Of course, for the intellectually oriented there are the so-called 'art films' in which the hero and heroine mumble two words, between gaps of silence. The other girl or man causes all the complications. Incest, lesbianism, adultery or various forms of social injustice are the raw material on which the theme is based but one is expected to appreciate the 'realism' of the film even if one had been bored to death while watching it!

60. *Some Stray Thoughts on Boxers*

Like millions of people all over the world I enjoy watching the World Heavy Weight Boxing Championship whenever I have the time and opportunity. Over the years (they have become a part of my nostalgic subconscious) I had watched these to the extent possible or at least been excited to hear accounts of great matches that have become the folklore of boxing.

It was only in the first decade of the last century that a person of African origin was allowed to take part in this sport. Jack Johnson knocked out Tony Burns in Sydney in 1908, to become the world heavy weight champion.

It was a great moment for African Americans. But Jack Johnson's contempt for whites, which manifested itself in his compulsive conquests of many white women (including two as wives) and his style of life tarnished his reputation and brought his career to an end even though he had managed to demolish in 1919 at Reno, 'the great white hope' Jeffries who had been brought with the sole purpose of defeating him.

I heard about the inspiring fights of Jack Dempsey (knocking down Firpo seven times in the first round) who was World Champion from 1919 to 1926, having knocked out Jess Willard in 1919 to claim the title, his flirtation with Hollywood and friendship with Charles Chaplin and Douglas Fairbanks.

There were other champions after that, like Tunney, but the man who conquered the world's imagination was Joe Louis, who bestrode the ring like a Colossus for 12 years, and whose devastating left hook is still considered the most lethal punch in boxing history. His many victories (Billy Cohn, Max Baer, Joe Walcott) have become the stuff of legend. He retired unbeaten in 1949. (Joe Louis would have to be regarded as undefeated though when he returned to the Ring in 1949 for financial reasons, he lost to Ezzard Charles, as age and lack of practice went against him.) His defeat at the hands of a man he would have obliterated in the first round years earlier is a lesson to all sportsmen not to return to any sport after a gap of time whatever be the provocation. In his last days he was a doorman in one of New York's Night Clubs—a pathetic contrast to his image as 'the Brown Bomber' (as he had been called) knocking out a succession of great boxers one after another at his peak.

About 50 boxers have become world heavy weight champions since the inception of the sport but only a handful can be referred to as all-time greats and Joe Louis heads the list.

Rocky Marciano defeated Joe Walcott in 1952 in Philadelphia and became the champion. When he suddenly quit the ring in 1956, he remained undefeated. The power and speed of his punches and his aggression gained him a place among the all-time greats, though to a large extent a well-orchestrated propaganda influenced public opinion.

Muhammed Ali became World Heavy Weight Champion three times. Despite several handicaps (e.g the Vietnam controversy). Ali, with his rope-a-dope trick, floated like a butterfly and stung like a bee, defeating a succession of boxers like Liston, Frazier and Foreman.

I still vividly remember watching on TV one cold morning in 1974 his historic fight in Kinshasa with Foreman, with my four-year-old son, who lustily cheered Ali's victory, sharing my thrill.

It is against this scenario that one must view the ignominious end of the controversial career of Mike Tyson, the youngest ever to become World Heavy Weight Champion. Though he appeared to have a bright future, his maniacal aggression, the conviction for rape and cannibalistic acts, denied him a place among the all-time greats mentioned above. The massacre in Memphis, at the hands of Leonard Lennox only underscores this conclusion. Though it is not considered prudent to compare boxers of different eras, none can dispute that Joe Louis was the greatest of them all.

61. *'Giants' of Yore*

There is a tendency on the part of earlier generations, while comparing the best in any field of human endeavour, with the best of our era, to refer to the former as relatively far superior. This in turn elicits a patronizing 'why bother to contradict them and enlighten them about the champions of our age' response from people of today. But even allowing a wide margin for nostalgia and subjective views, I am inclined to believe that there has been a universal lowering of standards in all fields, e.g. science, poetry, sports, movies and music, though ironically our quality of life has improved enormously, thanks to vast advances in science and technology.

Let me explain what I mean by this. We have to admit that there has been no erosion of human intelligence, talent and creativity just to name a few significant qualities. But at the same time we cannot deny that 'genius' and 'individual excellence' are not valued and respected now, as in the previous generations resulting in a lack of outstanding and exceptional people in all fields.

Let us first take a look at science, with say 1970 as the dividing line. There is no comparison between the calibre of scientists before that date, and those who came later. Good work was continuing to be performed and new inventions were continuing to improve our quality of life, but there were no great physicists like Einstein, Planck, Bohr, Rutherford, Dirac, Heisenberg, Schrodinger, Chadwick and Pauli, chemists like Pouling, Curie, Kendrew, Fishcer, Sanger, Robinson, Perutz, Langmuir and Urey and physiologists like Fleming, Medawar, Crick, Watson, Sherrington, Landsteiner, Banting, Hodgkin, Kendall and Huxley. (Scientists like Hawking and Penrose of this generation are of the same class but they are exceptions. Even Chandrasekhar got the Nobel Prize for work done before 1950.)

Take poetry, the twentieth century is a desert with just a few flowers, e.g. Yeats, Eliot, Dylan Thomas and Masefield when compared to the gardens of Miltonic splendour of the previous centuries with flowers of every hue and fragrance and fruits of every shape and taste worthy of paradise and fed by nectar running from Shakespeare's age in the sixteenth century to Tennyson's time.

Let us switch to sports, taking at random, cricket, tennis and boxing. Is there any one now who is of the class of Budge, Perry, Tilden Gonzales and Laver. After the era of Connors, Borg and Mckinroe there has been a huge void with the sole exception of Sampras. Boxing, which could once boast of names like Joe Louis, Rocky Mariciano and Jack Dempsey has no such colossus today. Even Mike Tyson has faded away ignominiously into oblivion, and there is no Bradman or Hammond Lindwall or Lilee. O'Rielly or Laker in Cricket. Even Tendulkar has miles to go before being called as legend.

The Golden age of Hollywood is over. There is no Clark Gable, Gary Cooper, Frederick March, Ronald Coleman, Errol Flynn or Tyrone Power. Nicholas Cage, John Travolta, Harrison Ford and Bruce Willis do not rise to the dizzy heights of emotion. Even the so-called best actors Robert De Nero or Dustin Hoffman cannot set the screen on fire like Lawrence Olivier or John Gielgud, as fantastic special effects and trick photography using advanced computer technology steal the thunder leaving an actor with no initiative or scope for displaying his own ability.

Let us go to Chennai (Madras) to review the local music situation. More 'sabhas' (halls exclusively devoted to classical music) have mushroomed and many youngsters have entered the field. But I would like to go back in a 'time machine' to the period when Semmangudi, Ariyakudi, GNB, Madurai Mani Iyer and Chembhai were enthralling audiences in different parts of the city.

Yes there were 'giants' in those days.

62. *One's Favourite City*

Every person has his or her favourite city in the world. No doubt the city where one was born, spent one's childhood, and gone to school occupies a pride of place in one's memories. It is the natural inclination of the human mind to fondly recollect happy memories from past events with nostalgia. Let us first define the characteristics that would make one classify a city as 'great', though one's subjective views count more when asked about one's favourite city! These are listed below, though the order is not indicative of the relative superiority of any one criterion.

Many would be inclined to regard area and population as major criteria, compelling us to consider large cities like New York, London, Los Angeles, Paris and Tokyo, to name a few. By the same token it would be difficult to ignore even New Delhi and Bombay.

Extremely beautiful and quiet little towns like Interlaken in Switzerland, Banf in Canada, La Jolla in America and Lusaka in Africa may be considered favourite cities by a few, even when they lack the above characteristics and are known only for their 'heavenly beauty'. But then should we not judge all cities by the quality of life they offer to the common man by way of easy availability of transportation and communication facilities rather than the world famous products sold by their shops or the Porches and the BMWs that cruise down their streets.

In terms of sheer magnitude of human achievement, New York would be the leader, making one wonder how man had ever been able to build those skyscrapers marking the Manhattan skyline, rivalled only by the giddy free-ways of Los Angeles that defy gravity!

Another criterion would be the historic fame of a city. London, Rome and New Delhi would fall under this category whereas, New York would take the first position for technological advancement and for being the financial capital of the world, and Los Angeles would have pre-eminence as a city with the largest number of freeways and motor vehicles. New York, London and Paris would also have to be ranked first for their fine museums and art galleries but London, Rome and Paris would outshine all American cities in respect of tradition and cultural heritage. Cities like New Delhi, Athens and Rome also would have to be included in this last group.

New York is said to never 'sleep'. It sustains a level of excitement and a pace of life which is to say the least staggering. One would have to also include Las Vegas, whose neon signs turn night into day and whose casinos churn out millionaires every night, Tokyo which has more 'night-clubs' than Paris and Rome combined, and Bangkok devoted to the worship of Aphrodite and Bacchus would also have to be included in this group. But then, New York, like so many other big cities, can also be intimidating, impersonal and insulting, when it shows you its violent and ugly face.

Thus, one's favourite city would necessarily be subjective, though some of the criteria discussed above would definitely add 'weightage'.

To me it must have some measure of all the criteria mentioned earlier but a few additional qualities—a harmonious blend of the old and the new, of tradition and modernity reflected in each and every aspect of the city, and above all three elusive qualities—style, dignity and romance. London alone has all these and every visit to that great Metropolis only strengthens that conviction. London steeped in history, has also 'class'. London to me is Sherlock Holmes and Charles Dickens, Harrods and Selfridges, Saville Row and Harley Street, not to mention Wimbledon and Ascot, a rich and wide tapestry that represents all the triumphs of man on this little planet of ours.

As Samuel Johnson had said

> when a man is tired of London, he is tired of life; for there is in London all that life can afford.

63. *What Is It About Japan?*

There is an apocryphal anecdote about a Japanese gentleman who had been invited in the 1950s by an American to his house along with a few other friends of various nationalities. The American host was taking his guests around the house simultaneously showing them various gadgets. He showed them the Grundig tape-recorder, and the Telefunken television made in Germany, the Kodak and Zeiss cameras made in America and Germany respectively; and the Rolex Swiss watch, and the wedgewood crockery from England. Lastly, he pointed out with pride to the Chrysler and Buick both made in America parked outside. He finally took out a small paper fan and addressing the Japanese guest said 'This, my dear friend, comes from your country, a jibe that indicated in no uncertain manner that Japan was capable of making only such small insignificant things.' The Japanese guest bore the insult with silent dignity but he had already planned in his own mind the future course of action.

Years rolled by and our American happened to visit Tokyo, and was invited by the same gentleman to his house along with a few other friends from different countries. It was his turn to take the guests around his house, he had been waiting for such an opportunity for years.

With 'modest pride' he showed them the Sony 'television and the Home Theatre system'; the latest Nikon camera, the Toyota Lexus which has knocked out almost every luxury car, not to mention the gas-guzzling American Chryslers and Buicks; the Seiko Chronometer which has became synonymous with accuracy for time keeping, and the shining Noritake crockery that has outclassed Wedgewood or Royal Doulton (except in the eyes of some Westernized oriental gentlemen!) Then he pointed out to a framed poster of the Niagara falls telling the American, 'this, my dear friend is from your country' (the frame by the way was made in Japan!) That Japanese gentleman was Akiro Morita who founded the Sony empire.

There is another incident which underscores what I have described above. A friend of mine had taken his American car for attending to a minor repair at a local gas-station in Los Angeles. He casually asked the owner whether he would advise people to buy American or Japanese cars. The latter replied that had he bought a Japanese car he would not have had to bring the car to his gas-station for repair because the cars made in japan never give trouble for years—whereas their Leviathan counterparts from Detroit need attention for some problem or the other every week! (thus demolishing the theory of some people who do not understand Japan that the country is good only at 'copying' but not making 'original' things). If Bob Hope who once in disgust dropped a defective pen in one of his movies muttering 'made in japan' utters such a line again, the joke would be on 'Him'. How ironical it is that today all the movies of Bob Hope are seen on Japanese made TVs all over America!

Yet another story concerns a visitor to America who had been taken to a departmental store by his host. He wanted to buy a tape-recorder and a camera. The salesman showed him the latest Sony tape-recorder and a Nikon 'top of the line' camera. Our visitor told the salesman that he was particular about buying only an American tape-recorder and camera. The salesman remarked to his friend that the visitor must be joking because it had been ages since people had stopped buying American cameras and tape-recorders!

Then the Japanese started buying up 'real estate' all over the west coast. The 'yen' became one of the strongest currencies and Japan became the biggest creditor nation lending astronomical sums of money to countries like Indonesia. In terms of GDP, total number of computers, television sets, automobiles, etc., it has become second only to America.

In fact, America itself owes Japan billions of dollors. Considering the comparative size and lack of resources, Japan has to be ranked ahead of any country in the world!

But then came the news from Japan of mismanagement of banks, the erosion of concept of loyalty to a single company and the necessity to devalue the yen, all of which seemed to indicate that Japan was heading for a recession making some people who have an obsessive admiration for America gloat over what they regarded would be a permanent state of affairs.

But as one of the world's best analytical journals has rightly pointed out, any talk of Japan going downhill would be too hasty and erroneous. Many times in the past Japan had displayed such tendencies and trends only to bounce back triumphantly to knock out competition in all fields. In fact, Japan deliberately seems to be resorting to such a pattern of behaviour!

My nephew who recently visited Japan was humorously remarking that even in rest rooms (toilets) Japan has reached a level of sophistication that no other country has; apparently near every toiled bowl there is a panel of buttons. By pressing various buttons you can have any scenery of your choice, the Niagara falls, the Himalayas or the Grand Canyon. And for the sick there is the added facility to analyse then and there itself a sample of the stools even before the person leaves the rest room, not to mention that for the fastidious the water suddenly gushes out in a spout and cleans the physiological region involved within seconds.

He added that every car in Japan has satellite global communication system—a feat not even America has yet achieved. Therefore, should it come as a surprise to any of us if today the world watches all entertainment on Japanese TV screens, listens to music played on Japanese systems and roads all over the world are jammed with Japanese cars. I cannot resist repeating that old joke about turning America upside down only to find words 'Made in Japan'!

64. *On National Integration*

When the All India Services were restructured to suit the Nation's needs following independence (they had been known as the Indian Civil Service earlier) one of the provisions introduced was to send an officer hailing from one part of the country, say Rajasthan, to another, say Kerala. It was hoped that such a move would promote national integration over the years. It is time to review the manner in which this administrative measure has achieved the purpose.

Anyway, I must mention at this point some of the biases and aberrations that have already been present in our national psyche.

Firstly, to the people belonging to the northern part of the country any one hailing from any one of the four southern states was a 'Madrasi' whether he came from Tamil Nadu or Karnataka! There was a total inability to distinguish between the four major languages, notwithstanding the fact that even in the days of the Raj people from the south had been making a genuine attempt to learn Hindi or Bengali, as the case may be, thanks to the relatively greater mobility of people from the south to the north to take up jobs and a desire to see Hindi movies, which even college students in the south considered 'fashionable'.

However, I have yet to see even till today a conscious attempt on the part of a person from Bhopal wanting to see a Telugu or Tamil movie. While on the subject of movies I cannot resist pointing out the rather obnoxious habit of a popular Hindi comedian, whose own sense of humour is rather low, meriting perhaps a two or three on a scale of one to ten of saying 'Ayyayyao' every five minutes supposedly refferring to the south Indian manner of speaking (which again makes me recollect a party I had attended at which a certain Punjabi gentleman asked the Tamilian sitting next to him, as to why when asked to spell 'moon', Tamilians say 'M-yo-yo-n' to which the Tamilian retorted by stating that it was precisely because Punjabis ask Tamilians why they were wrongly saying 'satation' instead of 'station' and 'sachool' instead of 'school'! I don't remember whether it was the same Punjabi who asked why Tamilians were fond of lapping up 'rasam' from the elbow as it flows from the fingers downwards to which the same Tamilian replied that he also could not understand why Punjabs tear their *nan* or *roti* by holding it firmly between their knees. There is also the complexion syndrome according to which south Indians are supposed to be dark whereas north Indians are fair. This conveniently ignores the fact that Vaijantimala, Hema Malini, Rekha and Sridevi dominated the Hindi screen for five decades sending the head of every north Indians male spinning, like a gyroscope. Every Carnatic musician can render *kritis* in Hindustani *ragas* with infinite ease. The Meera *bhajans* of M.S. Subbulakshmi and the great meditative openings of Semmangudi or GNB are too well known to be mentioned. On the other hand, one cannot name a single Hindustani classical musician rendering a *kriti* in Carnatic music, say in Hindolam (Rag Malkhaus in Hindustani music). In fact, most north Indians express a view that Carnatic music is too 'technical' and cannot be learnt—a load of crap disaproved by men like Higgins, the Connecticut Yankee who could sing *Siva Siva Yana Rada* like a seasoned Carnatic musician at the Madras Music Academy!

Getting back to the All India Services, the officers do have to pass a preliminary examination at the beginning of their career. In as much as the Review Board has a few members whose knowledge of the local language is not their 'strong point' the candidate can always scrape through. There is no review at any other stage to assess the knowledge of Telugu or Tamil except the mandatory requirement of issuing circulares in the local language. English always comes to the rescue in day-to-day conversations and the officer can 'muddle through'. But as long as a north Indian officer posted to Andhra Pradesh keeps saying 'idilo' for *deenilo* or *adilo* for *daanilo* no progress can be deemed to have been made. No complainant or petitioner will have the full satisfaction of having his complaint understood. Hence what is required is not the formality of passing an exam or implementing a circular, but a certain willingness to overcome mental blocks and cultivating a genuine desire to learn the language of the place to where one is posted so that true integration with the people there is possible to understand their problem. We expect only rudimentary knowledge of Telugu, not a great insight into Potana or Srinatha.

65. *The Mind of the Terrorist*

It was Thomas De Quincey who had pointed out that the intention of Shakespeare in writing a play like *Macbeth* was to show that when an act of murder is committed there is in the murderer's mind a living hell created by powerful emotions, such as jealousy and ambition. In contrast, the usual murder story is concerned only with the question of finding out the identity of the murderer and is, therefore, of little interest to the poet.

The relevance of De Quincey's observation to the subject under discussion may not be immediately obvious but will become so as we develop the theme.

The assassin or terrorist of today is different from a Shakespearean hero. An assassin kills for mercenary reasons though in a few ambition or greed provides the motivation.

The terrorist on the other hand is a horse of a different colour. His identity is known only to very few members of some fanatical organization (to which he belongs) whose security measures would be the envy of any government agency.

Two additional factors, which further complicate the issue are that the terrorist is filled with a fanatical zeal and is prepared to die for a cause.

All the arsenal which science and technology have at their disposal will not enable us to fix the identity, or anticipate the action, of the unknown terrorist moving in anonymity.

In the last sixteen months or so there has been world-wide increase in awareness of the threat from terrorism. Irrespective of earlier perceptions, which might have differed considerably from nation to nation, all countries, save a lunatic fringe, have now become united in their condemnation of terrorism, though the methods suggested to counter it might vary.

A second question that has recently become the focus of debate is the anticipation of a terrorist attack. There is no point in blaming intelligence agencies, as their operations are not all-pervasive and there are limits imposed by the very nature of democratic societies.

Then there is the major question of how to prevent a terrorist activity inside an aeroplane—whether it is going to be hijacked for being used as a missile to destroy a famous structure or for holding passengers as hostage.

Hundreds of suggestions have been put forth mostly centred on searching/checking of passengers/baggage carried in the cabin. The basic principle is to make security checks more intense so as to eliminate the possibility of an attack inside the aircraft. One organization has decided that henceforth liquor would be poured in plastic bottles as a broken glass bottle could be turned into a lethal weapon. Reacting to this, one airline wondered about the bottles of alcohol purchased in duty-free shops which passengers can take into the cabin. Should not glass be replaced by plastic there also? But then where does one draw the line? The object chosen by a terrorist to be used as a lethal weapon is known only to him. And there are inside an aircraft hundreds of items, any one of which can suit his purpose, e.g. foodtrays attached to the seats; handles of mini-televisions; equipment inside 'first-aid kits', beverages that can be made racket scalding hot in a few minutes; or even an extra long key or a tennis racket. In fact any object can be 'turned into a lethal weapon' by a resourceful and imaginative terrorist.

When an aeroplane is flying at an altitude of 35,000 feet at a speed of 500 miles an hour, with no chance of getting any help from outside, all the ideal ingredients necessary for a hijacker to destroy a famous landmark or carry out any other nefarious plan are readily available.

It is sad, unfortunate and pathetic that our human race, which can boast of having been able to conquer the environment in so many ways, and, has been able to erect engineering marvels such as the World Trade Center towers and invent the aeroplane, can itself sink to the depths of degradation in producing perverted maniacs who are able to destroy some of the greatest monuments to human dignity and pride on this planet!

As David Attenborough said about mankind

> No species has ever had such wholesale control over everything on earth, living or dead. That lays upon us, whether we like it or not, an awesome responsibility. In our hands lies now not only our own future but that of all living creatures with whom we share the earth.

Let us hope that our prayers will be heard by a benevolent God who will allow wiser counsels to prevail and protect the human race from destroying itself.

66. Frisking below the Belt

Following the destruction of the twin towers of the World Trade Center in New York there has been a realization that all conventional security measures are not adequate enough for protection against determined 'terrorists' who plan their operation meticulously and execute it with thoroughness, choosing the target and the time of attack under conditions of utter anonymity. The human bomb attacks in West Asia which have become more frequent than before, the periodic hijacks of aircraft all over the world and the attacks on embassies and other important buildings which seem to occur with a certain regularity have not exactly infused confidence and optimism in people's minds.

But the fear-psychosis generated by these incidents, as evidenced by a steep decline in travel all over the world, has compelled nations to review their whole approach to and preparedness against 'terrorism'. For the first time in history there is a realization that 'terrorism' is a global threat which has to be tackled on a war-footing.

It is in this context that we must view an incident that occurred at the Hyderabad airport a few months ago when I was boarding an Indian Airlines flight bound for Chennai in the evening along with the former director of the Central Bureau of Investigation and a distinguished professor of criminal justices from a prestigious American university, who was going to Chennai to deliver a talk, ironically, on 'terrorism' at the American Center.

As in most other airports in the country, security at Hyderabad airport is now being handled by the Central Industrial Security Force and not by the state police. I do not want to go into the merits of this nor the considerations that had led the Central Government to take such a step. Suffice to say that it does not seem to be any improvement; on the contrary checking of hand baggage and personal 'frisking' are accompanied by a certain avoidable rudeness and characterized by an utter lack of rationality.

After the baggage had been screened, weighed and checked-in, we passed through security, as is the usual procedure. The hand baggages were placed on the conveyor belt for X-ray screening and we were directed to go to the personal 'frisking' area. Till that stage everything went off smoothly, though in view of the fact that the 'frisking' went off for a much longer time than would appear to be necessary, the accidental contact of the frisking officer's hands with a certain part of the anatomy produced a sexual sensation which was by no means essential or enjoyable under the circumstances.

It was at this stage that a member of the security staff who was frisking me observed that I was carrying in my hand 'A Dictionary of Shakespeare's Quotations'. He first muttered inaudibly and then fairly loudly that I should get the book 'tagged' at the place where the hand baggage, after screening by X-ray, was being retrieved. When I brought this to the notice of the people who were examining the hand baggage near the X-ray machine, I expected that at least at that stage, intelligence (pun intended) might dawn on the brains of those charged with the duty of scanning the hand baggage. On the contrary the person there was only too eager to put a tag a rubber band to which is tied a rectangular piece of cardboard duly stamped, completely 'enclosing' the book, containing the quotations of the greatest genius mankind has ever produced.

I imagined the Bard of Avon turning in his grave and muttering to himself the lines uttered by Macbeth in a different context: 'I am cabin'd, cribb'd, confined and bound in' or as Mark Antony said to Caesar's corpse) adding to it a touch of De Quincey) 'Pardon me o mighty poet, that I should make you endure, such torture in the hands of the ignorant'.

I have served in the Indian Police Service for 35 years and do appreciate the need for security and the fact that in enforcing it there can be no compromise. But there should be a rational basis to these measures and we should not be carried away and go to extremes.

67. *Vaastu—Queen of Pseudo-sciences*

In History's Catalogue of pseudo-sciences, fads and fallacies, the so-called Vaastu Sastra, which is being regarded as a science, or a science-cum-philosophy, occupies a pre-eminent place.

Its sweeping claims to being a holistic way of living in harmony with the forces of nature, its self-proclaimed ability to harness the potential of 'unknown' cosmic forces to improve the quality in any sphere of human life include altering the structure, design and location of buildings to enhance the bliss of conjugal life, particularly its obscene obsession with the bedroom—'Rati Kaksha', the room meant for love-making by manipulating the size, location, design and manner of utilization of the bed; to render advice to improve the taste of food by altering the location of the kitchen; and the internal distribution of the basins, sinks, taps and stoves; to offer baseless suggestions to owners of houses, apartments and office establishments about the manner in which toilets, kitchens and working places are to be arranged; and to top it all, to come out with the rather ridiculous theory that items of furniture should not be arranged in 'L' shape have absolutely no scientific basis!

Vaastu 'virus' rages unchecked infecting all those with whom it comes into contact, thus affecting a major portion of the population till the disease reaches epidemic proportions. The defenders of this faith include civil servants, politicians, actors, businessmen, sportsmen and housewives. The disease has now reached such an advanced stage that no cure is possible. Only immunization by sound education at an early stage in life could prevent this. Perhaps we can save future generations!

Vaastu has no relevance to our existence by any stretch of imagination, particularly in the age of Einstein's Relativity when we have irrefutable proof that time, distance and direction are all relative. How can any prudent person accept the concept of relative directions within a house or inside a street influencing his destiny?

Let us examine whether Vaastu meets the strict criteria of science. Unlike science it does not go into the 'how' of things. Nor is it concerned with what is universally understood by the terms 'objective evidence' or 'scientific proof'.

On the other hand its entire foundation rests on dogmatic assertions based on unwarranted assumptions such as (a) telephone can be kept in the east or north or south-east. But no water jug should be kept near the telephone. (b) Television should not be placed in the north-west or south-west corner. (c) Toilet should not be kept in the central portion of the apartment. An apartment having main doors to the south will experience trouble and so on and so forth. What is even more strange and amusing is that such theories are put forth with a certain degree of finality notwithstanding that they have no scientific basis. One wonders whether telephones and televisions were in existence when Vaastu was first developed!

Vaastu experts believe that there are five elements—wind, space, fire, water and earth, which work in unison. Evidently they have not heard of the periodic table, let alone the fact that these other entities can never be classified as elements in chemistry. In fact, all five are excellent examples of compounds/mixtures. Vaastu experts believe that the big five will create disharmony if no balance is maintained. What utter nonsense! For modern day educated people to allow such principles to guide their lives is an unpardonable crime.

Vaastu experts believe that all the problems of this country have their origin in the imperfect Vaastu of the Himalayas about which nothing can be done. Of course they conveniently forget that India is the cradle of civilization, the land which produced the *Mahabharata*, the *Ramayana*, the Vedas and the Upanishads. It is the land, which gave the world Carnatic music and some of the most exotic dance forms like the Bharatanatyam, Kuchipudi and Odissi. Are there in any other corner of the planet monuments of stone devoted to the worship of Aphrodite, like Khajuraho and Konark? No, it is absurd to blame the Himalayas and follow the fraudulent, bogus and blatantly nonsensical principles of a pseudo-science called Vaastu with the hope of making progress. Fortunately, the information age has come to us before we would have descended into chaos. Let us throw all books on Vaastu and other pseudo-sciences into a big fire, retain our sanity, and move forward to recapture our lost glory.

68. *The Tonsorial Debate*

Long ago before the birth of Christ there were a people opposing Israelites in ancient Palestine. They were materialistic and cruel, and lacked culture and exercised domination over the Israelites by virtue of their military might. They ill-treated them, overtaxed them and exploited their weakness in several ways. The Israelites suffered their plight silently.

But then a man was born among the Israelites, who had such incredible strength that his fame spread rapidly far and wide. Several times he single-handedly vanquished the Philistines in battle, striking panic in their hearts. When asked to choose a prize for killing a lion bare-handed. Samson, as he was named, chose a Philistine girl he was in love with as his bride. The bride's sister, who had also been secretly in love with Samson, was so hurt that she swore revenge and told the Philistines that she would help them to capture Samson. (By that time a brawl had taken place in the bride's house, just when the wedding preparations were on, and the bride got accidentally killed by a flying missiles—a spear.)

Delilah lured Samson to a silken tent in the desert and, using her 'quips and cranks and wanton wiles', asked Samson about the secret of his strength. In one weak moment he revealed that his strength lay in his hair. Mixing a sleeping potion in his drink, Delilah lulled him to sleep and cut off his mane before he woke up. When the Philistines came to capture him, he found himself helpless. Though the King of the Philistines gave his word to Delilah that no blade would touch Samson's skin and no blood would be shed, he had Samson blinded with the scalding heat of an iron poker, which was brought close to the eyes. Delilah came to know about Samson having been blinded only much later when she went to the grinding mill where Samson had been chained and put to hard labour.

Delilah's wrath turned against the Philistines and she decided to help Samson to take revenge on them. With the passing of time, Samson's hair grew unnoticed to its normal length, but Delilah convinced him that as he was blind, his strength would be of no avail without her help. On a particular day Samson was taken to the Pagan temple of the

Philistines. All the Philistines had gathered there to watch Samson getting humiliated. Delilah, who knew that the entire temple rested on two pillars, offered to whip Samson herself but cleverly guided him to those pillars. The king, who was in love with Delilah, suspected Delilar's plan, but it was too late. Samson pushed the pillars down and destroyed the temple and, along with it, the Philistines. He also died.

In Greek mythology there is a Gorgon called Medusa. For hair she had smakes, and anyone looking at her turned into a stone. In Hindu mythology the *jatajutam* or hair of Lord Shiva is the source of the Ganga.

Tales such as these have an allegorical significance which is not immediately apparent. For example, in the *Mahabharata*, since Dushashana pulled Draupadi by her hair before disrobing her, Bhima took a vow to wash Draupadi's hair in Dushashana's blood—a task he accomplished after killing him.

Of course, in the lyrical poetry of almost all languages playing with the beloved's hair is part of foreplay. As Richard Lovelace spoke about his sweetheart from prison:

> When love with unconfined wings
> Hovers within my gates,
> And my divine Althea brings
> To whisper at the grates;
> When I lie tangled in her hair
> And fettered to her eye
> The gods that wanton in the air
> Know no such liberty.

Coming to this unisex age when a million hairstyles are sported round the world, it may perhaps be desirable for some one occupying a high position, and who will be constantly in the public eye, to have a conventional hair style rather than improve upon that of the Beatles and create a tonsorial controversy to add to our innumerable problems, unless, the hair happens to cover some secret missile formula, the only one of which is in existence on his scalp!

69. *A Tale of Two Cities*

I visited Hyderabad for the first time in the winter of 1957. Hyderabad was an 'overgrown town' just emerging from the era of the Nizams into post-Independence India. Though it was famous for the splendour and opulence of a bygone era, the aristocracy of the Nawabs, its exquisite cuisine and mellifluous Urdu, I had not been in a position to appreciate those aspects at that stage, apart from a vague awareness of the fact that the Nizam had once been regarded as the richest man in the world. Many incidents (some real, some apocryphal) enhanced this image. My favourite story concerns a jeweller from abroad, who, having found no one rich enough to buy his gems, had come to Hyderabad. The Nizam, after looking at them, summoned his attendants to bring two trunks which were full of similar gems. The jeweller got the hint, but while leaving managed to prevent a paper-weight from falling. He had a look at it and reportedly fainted; that paper-weight is the famous 196-carat Jacob diamond which was receltly displayed at the Salar Jung Museum under-valued currently at Rs 475 crore!

Hyderabad in the early 1960s had only a few decent restaurants, hotels and movie houses and a small airport with some sort of transit facility. A visit to Tank Bund or Abids constituted the height of entertainment.

Today it is a large city, with very wide roads and beautiful parks occupying large areas, an international airport, many modern restaurants, posh hotels and a computer revolution thanks to good governance' as former US President Bill Clinton had put it. Yes, it has hundreds of other problems, but an effort is being made to solve them.

In Chennai (Madras), Luz Church Road, a street famous for some of India's greatest lawyers, ends at Alwarpet in one direction. (Luz Church Road was to lawyers in Madras what Harley Street was to doctors in London.) In fact, it is one of the well-known streets of Mylapore, named after the famous temple nearby. In an old Tamil movie, one lady is referred to as the daughter-in-law of a 'Mylapore advocate' an indication of status. Alwarpet had only a shop for repair of cycles, a shop selling soft drinks, and a barber's shop. Today there is a flyover, an intensive care hospital, a huge departmental store and several other shops and restaurants.

A walk from Alwarpet to Luz is a trip down 'memory lane'. In the old days there were just a few houses of the greatest lawyers, a church and a room where Ramanujan, the greatest mathematician of the twentieth century, had stayed; Luz corner was a modest place with a few shops. Mount Road was 'Fifth Avenue' with Jaffar's, Syed Bawker's and Connemera being the ultimate in ice creams, tailoring and hotels respectively. Today you cannot recognize Luz Church Road with its multistoreyed buildings (some houses have disappeared) and Luz Corner has become a major shopping centre (another flyover). Sprawling Chennai is bursting at its seams with more vehicles and people than it can handle. The quiet dignity and old world charm which were the essential hallmarks of Chennai have yielded to pace, excitement and all the trappings of a commercial metropolis, but also traffic congestion, pollution and administrative chaos!

The only redeeming feature is that Chennai retains its cultural image (mentioned by even Marco Polo) and the Music Academy is still the 'Wimbledon' of Carnatic music, the most complex musical system in the world. Chennai is not decaying, but then the Mylapore of Marco Polo has disappeared; nor do the walls of the Music Academy resound to the intricate 'swaras' of Semmangudi and the booming voice of GNB any more, though the mantle has fallen on a new generation of energetic youngsters. Mylapore Club is still there, but the silky tennis swing of Ramanathan Krishnan is not there.

70. *Exploitation of Women has Another Side*

> Women are the poetry of the world in the same sense as the stars are the poetry of heaven—clear, light-giving, harmonious they are the terrestrial planets that rule the destinies of mankind.
>
> HARGRAVE

There is a great deal of hue and cry all over the world about the exploitation of women by men, and the urgent necessity of liberating women from the chauvinistic environment of a male dominated society.

No doubt we would be exposing ourselves to the charge of intellectual dishonesty if we deny that there are many countries in which large sections of women are victims of unspeakable atrocities like dowry, slave-trade, wife-beating and physical mutilation. Social reform, legislation and enforcement are absolutely necessary to eradicate such evils. But hardcore feminists, instead of concentrating on such horrors, ironically cite a number of comparatively less serious issues in everyday life, going to the extent of even distorting or misinterpreting facts to suit their argument.

While expressing my sympathy for the plight of women belonging to the former category, I wish to state that this article is intended only to demolish the erroneous and extreme view expressed by the above-mentioned groups in certain types of movies, articles or books and not to hurt the feelings of millions of women who perhaps may not share such views.

Let us first take the question of large shopping malls (the most visible landmark) in the United States. Seven times as much floor space is devoted to women's personal items as to men's. Apart from that, more goods are bought for women who spend much more in almost every consumer category. This naturally gives them control over television programmes because they are controlled by sponsors. Women also watch more television programmes in every timeslot, a situation prevalent all over the world. No wonder women are in a position to depict their own sex as victims in most movies and television serials.

Feminists like to compare marriage to slavery for women. In America alone twenty-five million women every month read twenty romantic novels which fantasize marriage. This is true in respect of other countries also though the figures may vary. Does this mean that these twenty-five million women fantasize as their goal of love, a social contract involving their own slavery, for masochistic reasons?

Experimental drugs are usually tried on men. If the drug fails, the man dies. If the drug proves safe and useful it is naturally used to treat both women and men. In fact men have been used as guinea pigs in developing medical procedures and microwave ovens. (A man was in advertently cooked to death in such a trial.) Ironically, this was described as sexism since doctors had studied men. The fact that they had been used as guinea pigs was conveniently ignored!

A favourite theme of feminists is that marital traditions such as the father giving away the bride are a reflection of patriarchy. Actually the father is giving away his responsibility to protect his daughter. The word husband itself is derived from the germanic 'house' and the old Norse for 'bound' or 'bondage'. It also has its origin in words meaning a male kept for breeding! Shakespeare himself says this in '*Measure for Measure*':

> You can cut off a man's head if a man be a bachelor, sir, but if he be a married man no; for a married man is a woman's; to cut off a married man's head is to cut off a woman's head and I cannot cut off a woman's head.

71. *It is Man Who Needs Liberation*

Since time immemorial man has had to prove his ability to protect or provide for woman, if necessary, by taking all kinds of risks including death. There has been no such requirement for woman especially if her face could launch a thousand ships or the shape of her nose could change the course of history.

Let us now come to more fundamental issues, the biological conditions of men and women, and their social and matrimonial positions in the light of their individual behaviour traits.

At this very minute all over the world men are taking out women to restaurants and movies, buying them chocolates, flowers, perfumes, clothes and even engagement rings which women need not return should they not get married.

Nature made man biologically dependent on female beauty and woman dependent on his protection. But the world's most potent drug is female beauty. A man gets addicted to female beauty, youth and sex even more than to money power, alcohol or drugs and suffers withdrawal symptoms if they are not available for some reason—a fact only too well known to the daughters of Eve and the sisters of Delilah. Biology has given them the power to effortlessly endure sexual abstinence for long intervals of time because of child bearing responsibilities and other related hormonal factors—a power a woman can cunningly use to manipulate a man who has no such faculty.

This is why he temporarily loses his mind and makes an irrational decision to support her for life. No wonder Shakespeare says that many a man in love with a dimple 'makes the mistake of marrying the whole girl'.

Marriage is the price men pay to have sex. Sex is the price women have to pay to stay married. By the same token for every husband who demands sex as a right there are ten wives who withhold sexual favours as a punishment or for obtaining benefits—a state of affairs that has no doubt led to the institution of prostitution. Female beauty and sexual power are nature's marketing tools; the way it markets women for survival of genes.

Men are willing to give up money, kingdoms and empires or even go to war to attain the precious commodity of female beauty. It has never been necessary for women to rule Rome as they could manipulate Caesars. If from within a bedroom or behind a veil they could wield unbelievable sexual power, there was never any necessity for them to sit on a throne!

In modern society boys initiate dates and it is the girl's prerogative to refuse a boy's request whether on telephone or on the dance floor. The pill has freed girls from the fear of unwanted pregnancy while their awareness of their own capacity to experience unlimited orgasms has given them an unfair advantage over boys in the game of sex. A woman is always 'capable' though not necessarily 'willing' to receive a man, whereas a man cannot claim any such prowess even in the age of viagra, considering that the time of interaction is decided by the woman. As one prominent American comedian observed, 'When a women consents to have sex it is considered a sexual favour.' She is entitled to receive something in return. No such privilege is enjoyed by the man. If he refuses favours it serves no purpose for he only hurts himself.

Notwithstanding what sex manuals say, *Playboy* outsells *Playgirl* by hundred times, even if feminists would regard this as an example of man's exploitation of female nudity. They have no explanation for the utter indifference of women to *Playgirl* or even explicit senses depicting female nudity. Nor will feminists admit that a fascination for magazines like *Playboy* only indicates man's enslavement to female beauty. When a man exposes his body it is regarded as cheap exhibitionism and he may be even put in jail. When a woman exposes herself, she becomes a Miss Universe or a *Playboy* centrefold which earns her millions of rupees and even launches her on a movie career.

Having said all this we come to the conclusion that women's liberation has perhaps relevance only to those unfortunate persons whose historic position and national and social customs compel them to undergo all kinds of physical torture and abuse and severe forms of discrimination, which over the years have acquired the sanction of a civil code. Where comparatively equal opportunities for education, jobs, power, wealth and social influence exist, it is perhaps men more than women who need liberation from the tyranny of women's sexual power however subtly excercised.

72. *On Nicknames*

One habit of our fellowmen which amuses me is their tendency to refer to each other by all sorts of nicknames instead of the original names given at birth. Even more amusing is that very often these nicknames are not just simplified versions of the real name, for the sake of convenience, or given rationally on the basis of some performance in studies or sports at school or association with some incident. On the contrary, the person concerned cannot even explain the reason for the distortion of his name, and is quite willing to sail through life with it.

This tendency can be traced back to early childhood itself. The younger boy in a household who had been given the beautiful name of a God, say Vishwanath, or the term for some admirable virtue like Vidyasagar or Dhirender begins to be addressed as Chotu or Badey based on the relative age, or Vishi and Sagu or Dhiru. As time passes the distortion gets worse and unrecognisable having no correlation to the original name, i.e. Vyish, Sags and Byre.

Children at school deliberately give humiliating names to teachers like 'Elugubantu' (bear) for the maths teacher who is hairy, 'Navamasa Garbini' (a woman who is in the ninth month of pregnancy) for the civics master who has a huge belly, and 'Gudlagooba' (owl) for the history teacher who has very prominent eyeballs, and so on and so forth (all these teachers have respectable names chosen from our great epics).

While pardoning children for such antics, what should be of concern for all of us is the psychological process at work that seems universal and which eludes any explanation.

The nicknames defy any attempt to dislodge them and sometimes completely obliterate the original name. One example I can readily recall is the trouble I had to undergo to trace one 'Kikki' abroad for the sake of a visiting friend. Unfortunately, he himself had forgotten where 'Kikki' was working and could not readily recall his original name. He returned to India a disappointed man, having not met 'Kikki' ! There must be many more such instances, which readers may be able to recall.

In training institutions like those of the Police, where the cadets are put through a rigorous course of physical exercise (beyond the limits of human endurance?) the helpless trainees resort to a psychological compensatory mechanism, by referring to their physical instructors by various humiliating names/terms e.g. 'One-eyed Jack', 'Fatso', 'Hunchback', etc.

Male students in a school or college, use flattering names to refer to their female counterparts, e.g. 'Peach' or 'Chocolate' or 'Blue Robin' if the girl has a reputation for beauty, but 'barge-pole', 'skeleton', 'pumpkin', etc., in ease beauty or charm is not the strong point of the unfortunate victim. One tall girl whose name was Kamala was referred to as 'Talcum', an innovation that deserves praise.

An uncle of mine, whose speciality was pun, referred to 'Sherlock Holmes' as 'Sheerluck Holmes', and a small 'Venus De Milo' statue gifted to him by his son as 'Venus De Mylapore'. One dentist in Madras Migalani was described by him as a person who leaves no tooth unpulled, charging you heavily ('Pannu Migalaneeyadu', 'Dabbu Migalaneeyadu' respectively).

Sometimes, the nickname is a 'pet name' for a loved one, e.g. 'CLBDK (Cute Little Baby Darling Kitten) for one's young bride (though it is longer than the actual name or 'pooney kutti' (kitten) for the younger son and 'pooney' (cat) for the elder son, though the elder one had also been referred to as 'pooney kutti' when he had been the only baby, before the second one was born. Of course, the father has to be very careful not to address them in this fashion in public.

Sometimes people are referred to only by their initials. G.N.B., (G.N. Balasubramanian) or M.L.V. (M.L. Vasantha Kumari). This practice is prevalent in the south where even family names or first names are commonly used for referring to musicians and actors, e.g. Lalgudi (for Lalgudi Jayaraman) and Gummadi for (Gummadi Venkateswara Rao). These are accepted by the ordinary public and the artists.

Similarly, there is yet another harmless category; some people are generally known throughout life by certain names—Dodo, Cheta, Kummu, Daggi, etc., whose genesis cannot be traced.

However, the tendency of distortion of names is irrational and irritating and hence avoidable, but there is perhaps no harm, insofar as the intention is to indicate intimacy and introduce informality, or for the sake of humour and convenience. But where the motive is either to insult or humiliate or even reflect a patronising attitude, it may not be possible to defend the action. In fact, it has to be discouraged. As far as I am concerned I have not had any problem with people referring to me as Raves, or Ravas till now.